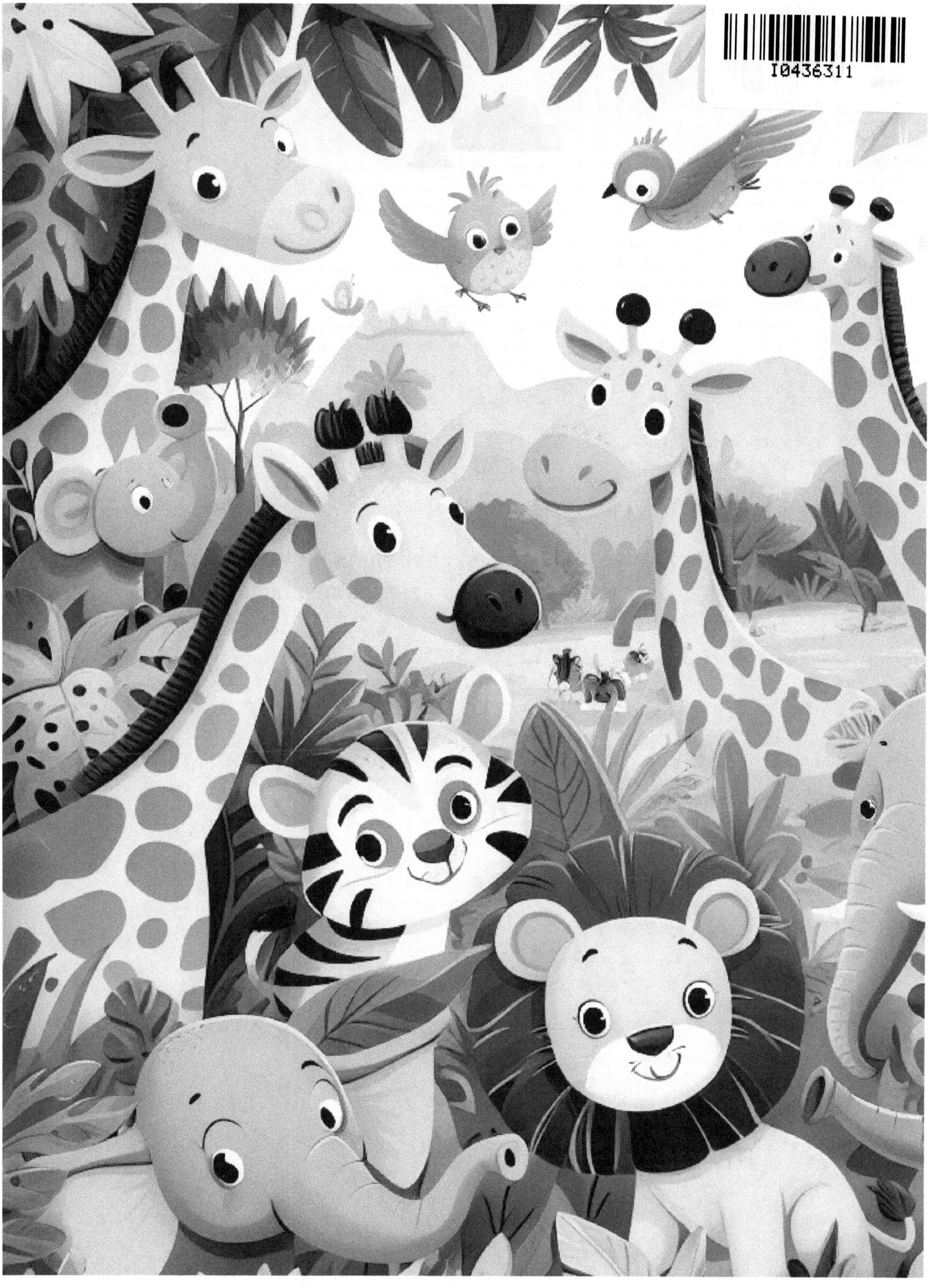

I am grateful to God for everything! And I believe that the meaning of life is to make sense of other lives. C.A., you are the meaning of my life.

Lov U

Ícaro e Arthur

2022

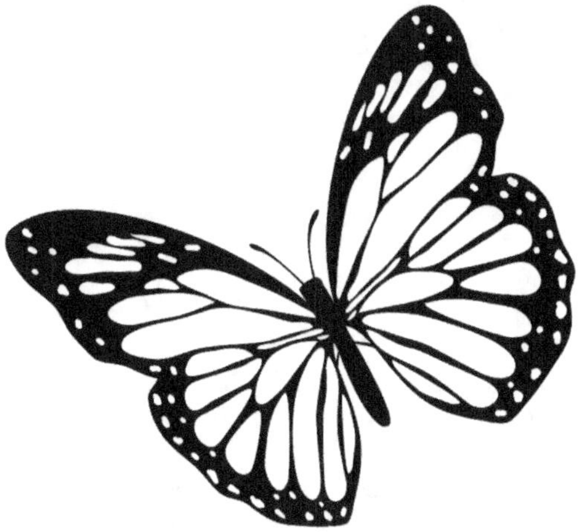

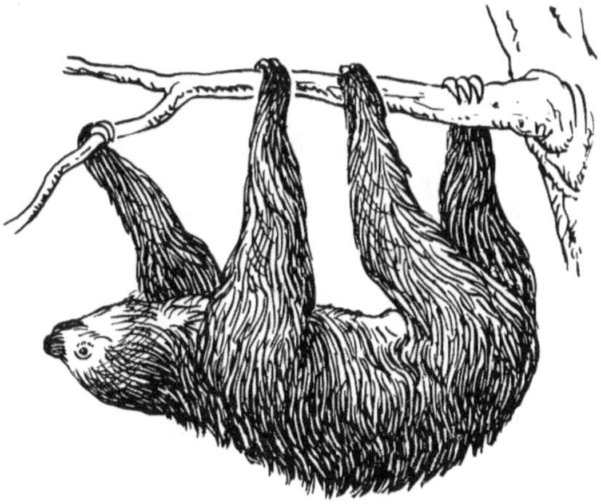

This Book Belongs to:

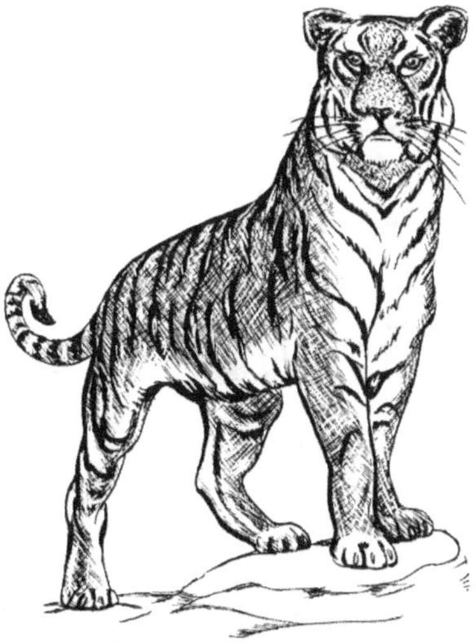

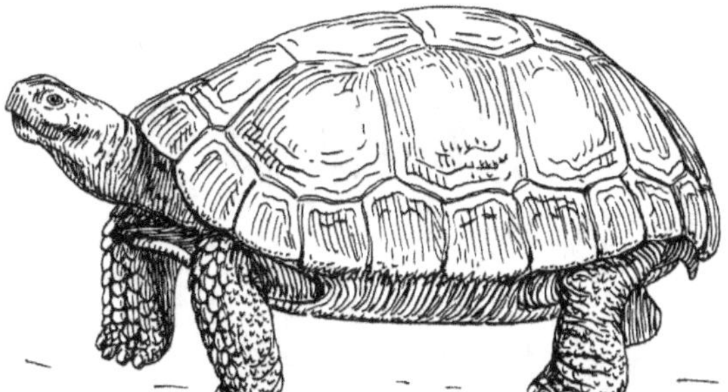

I.A.P. ©
Ícaro & Arthur publications

Test Color Page

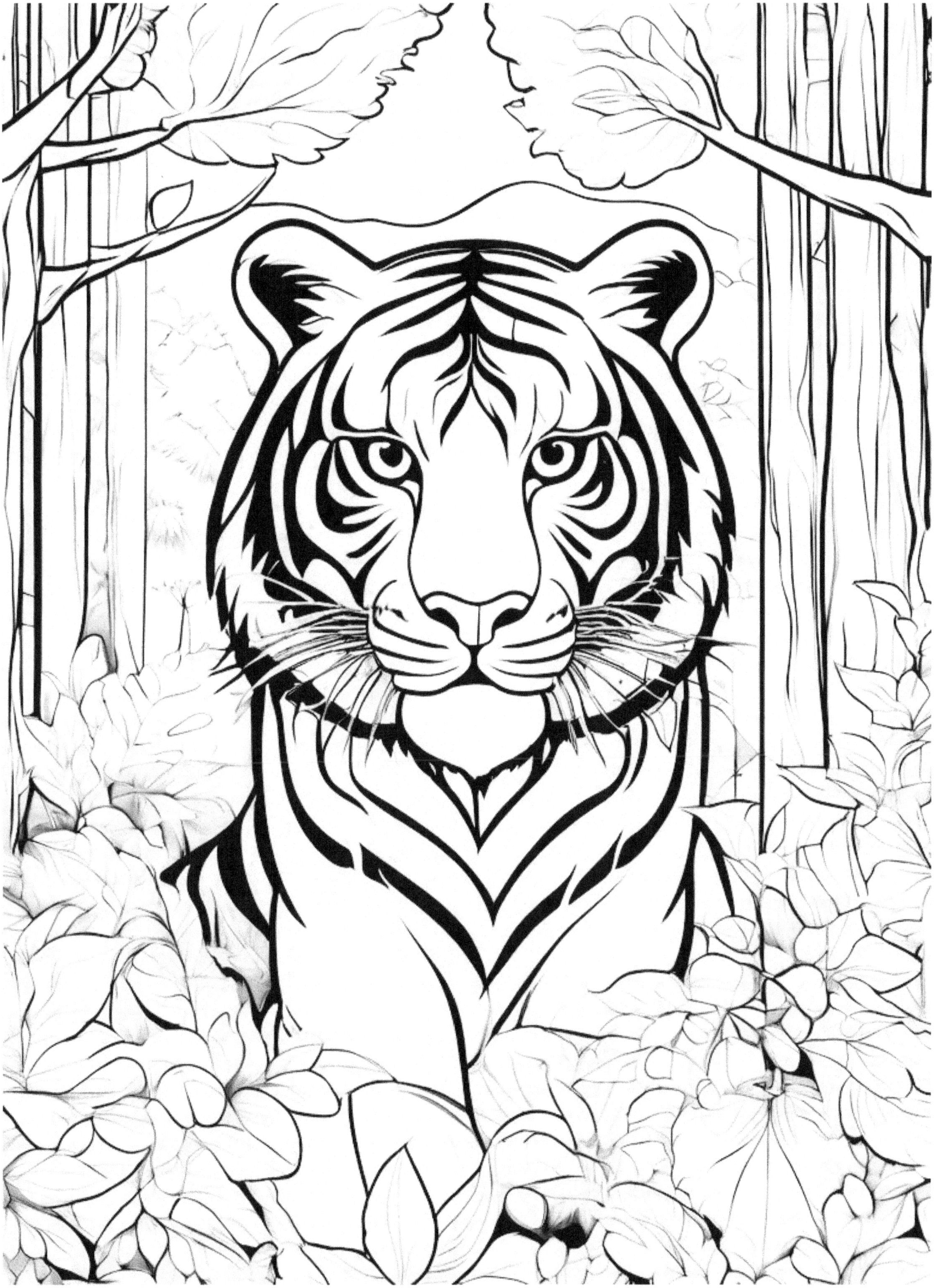

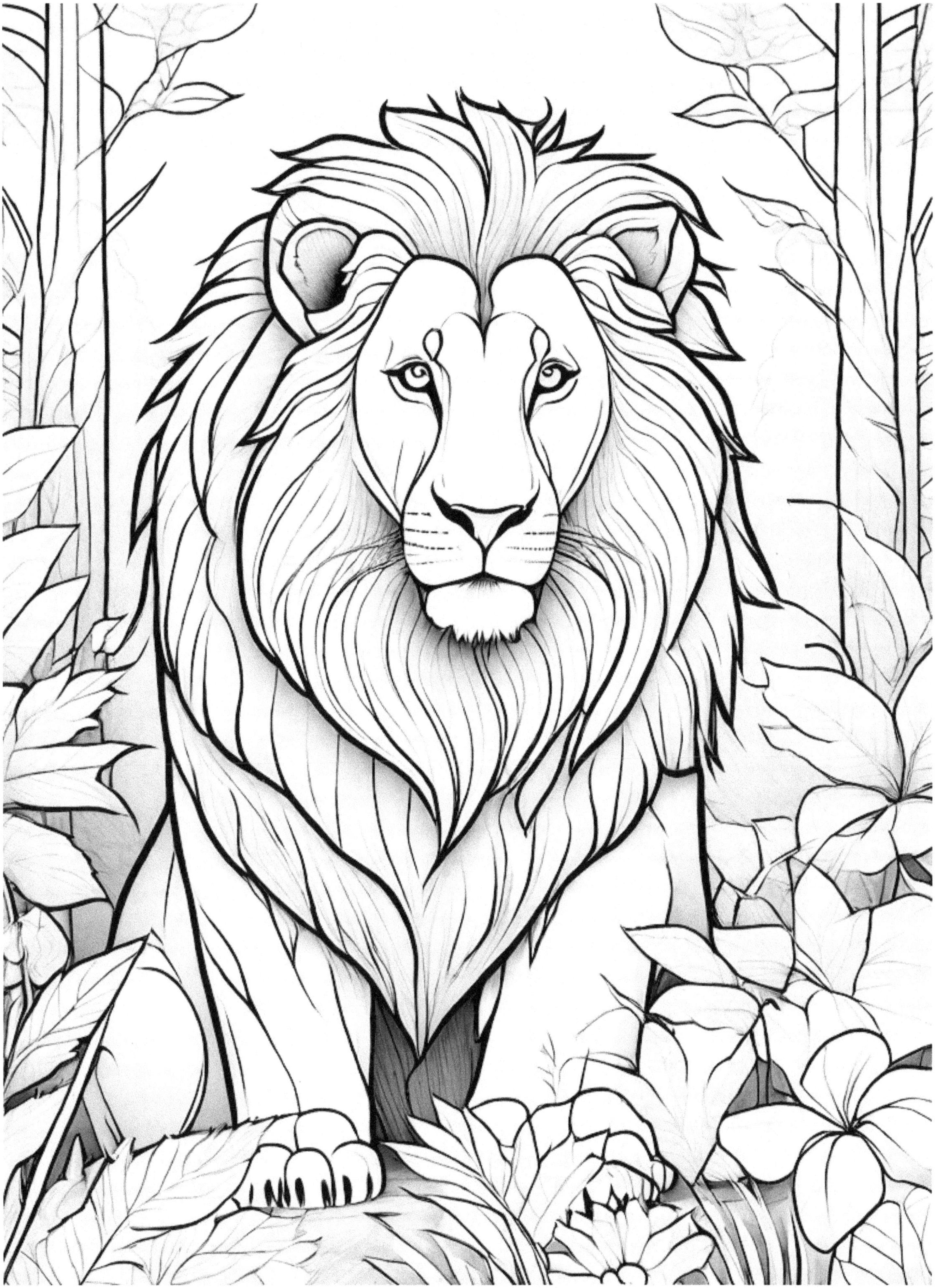

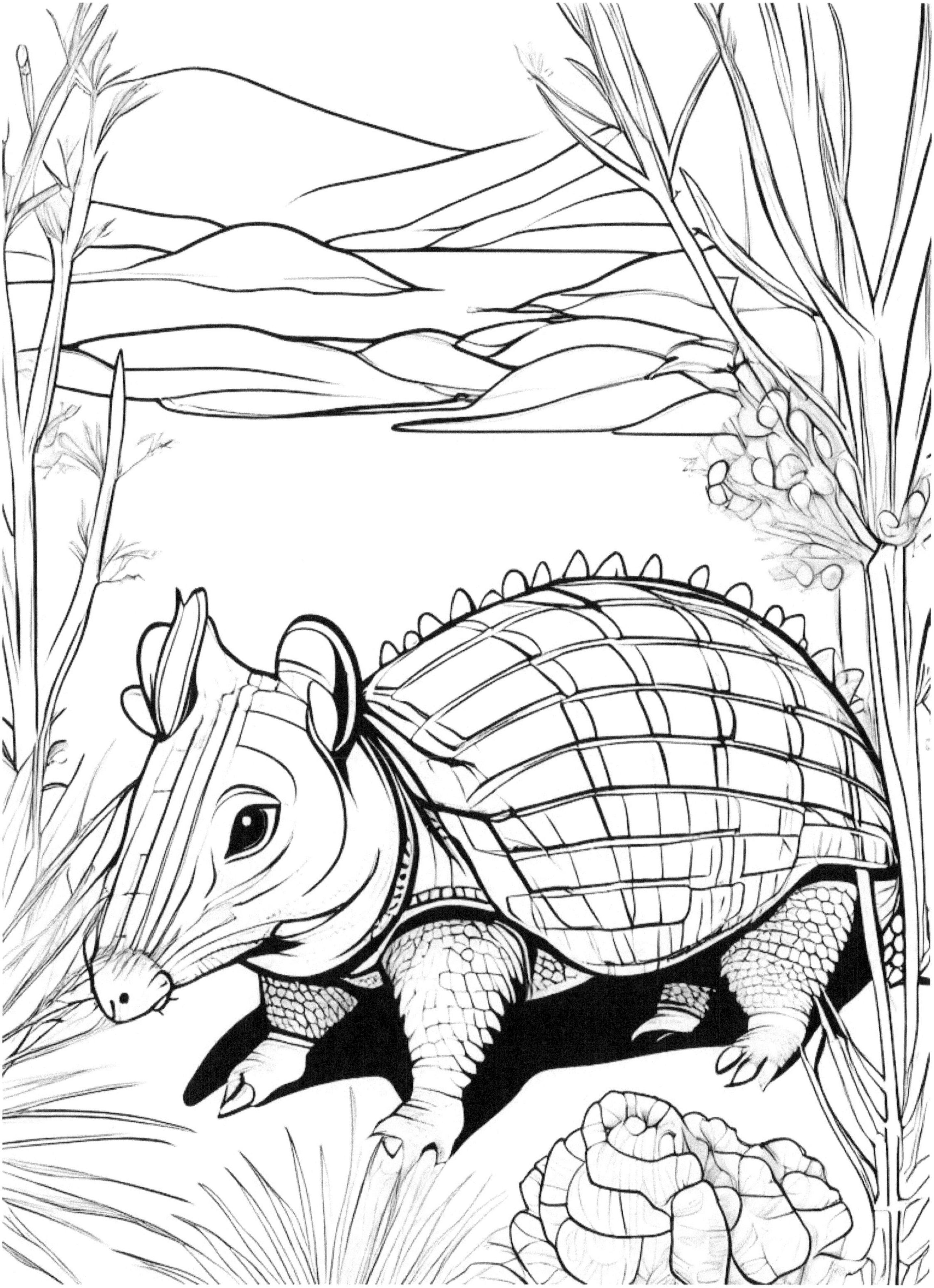

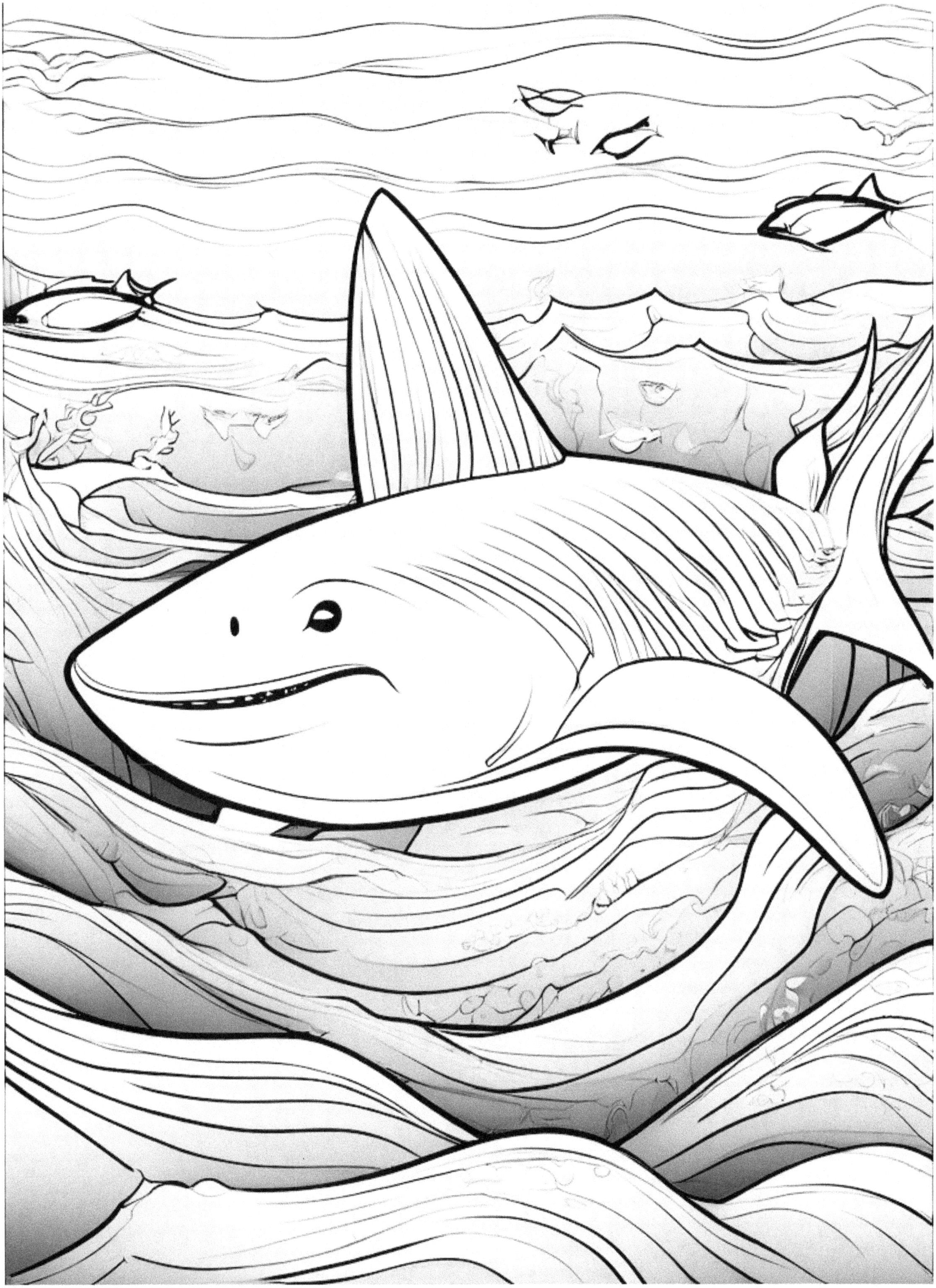

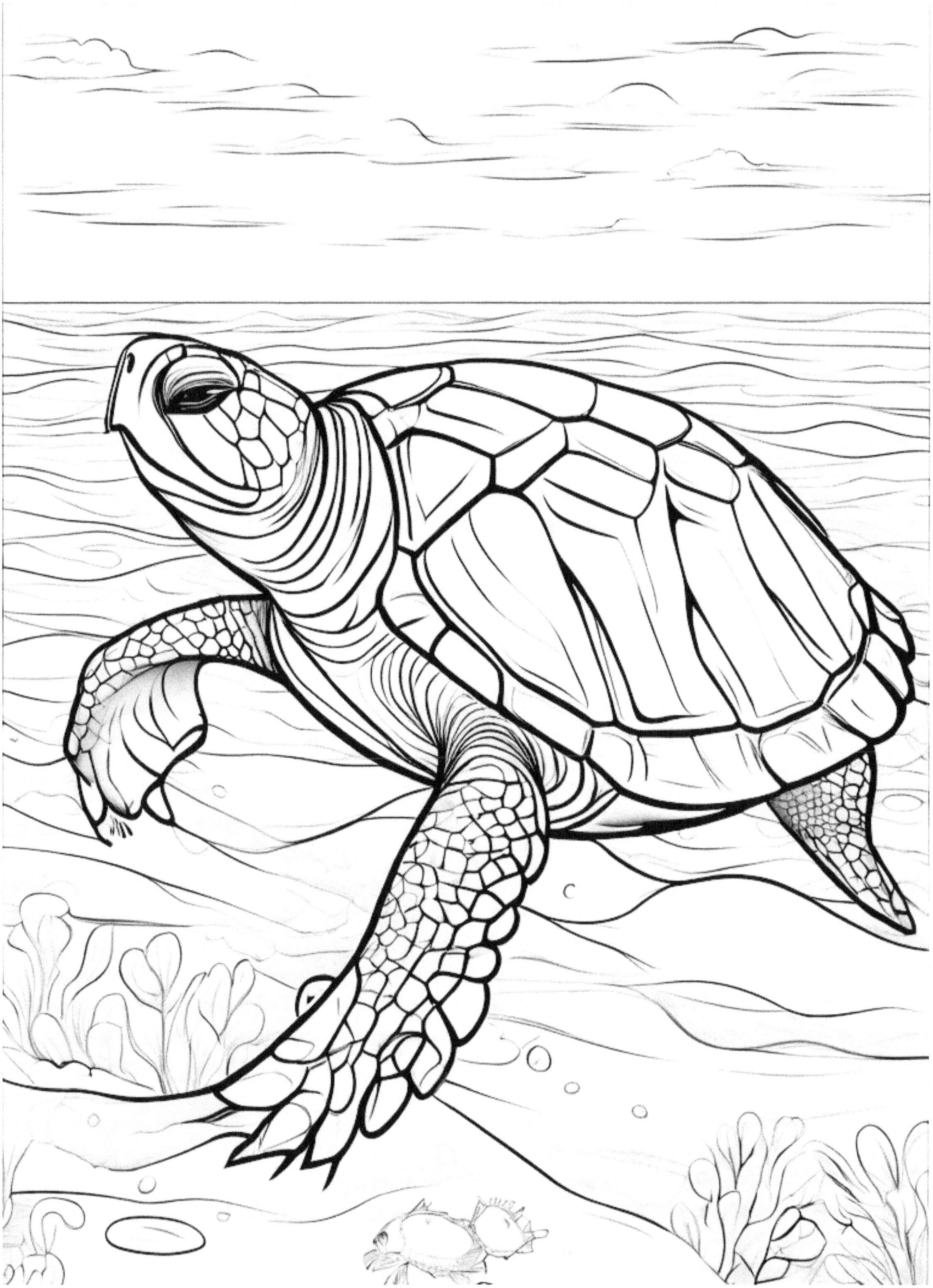

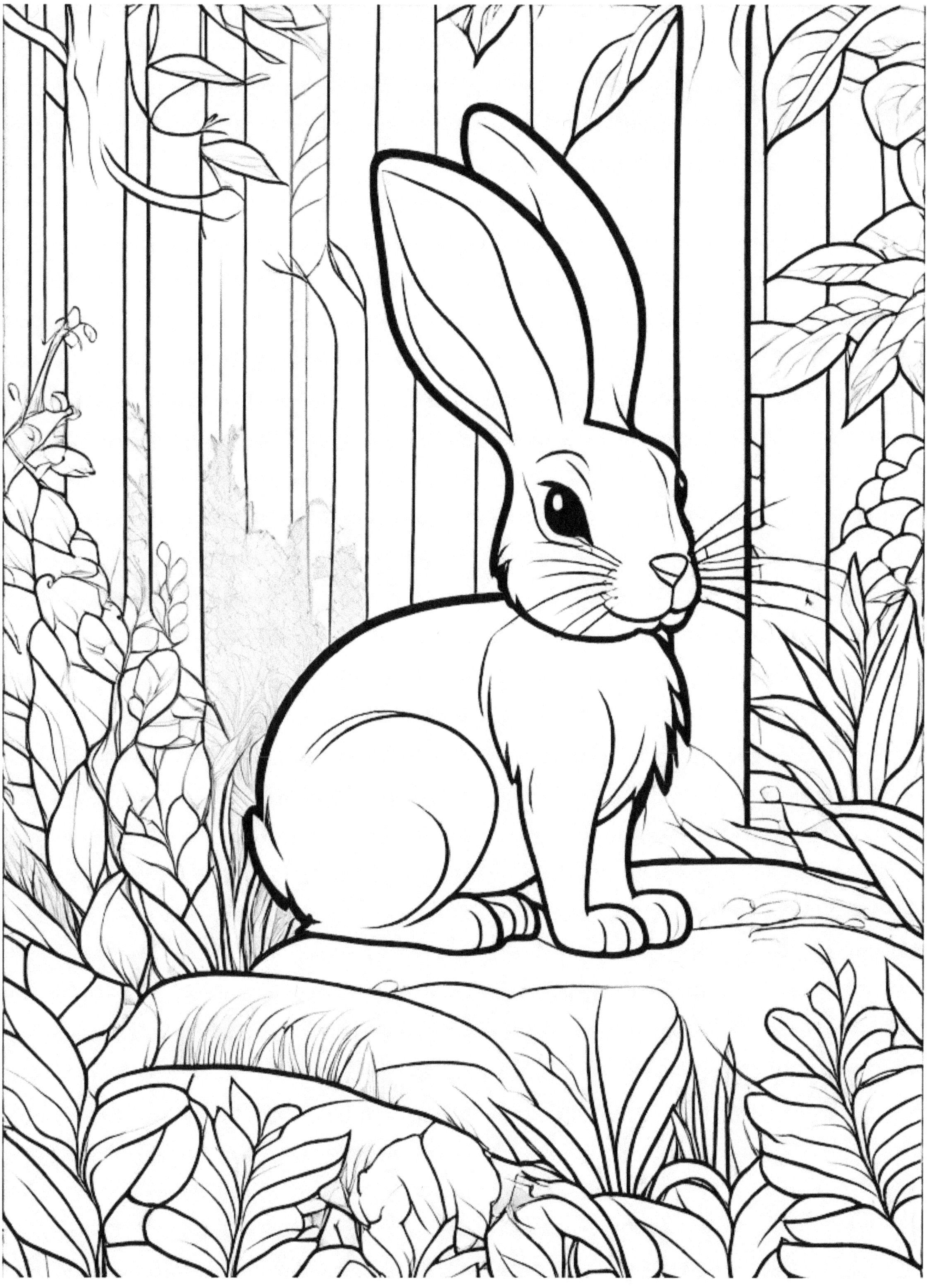

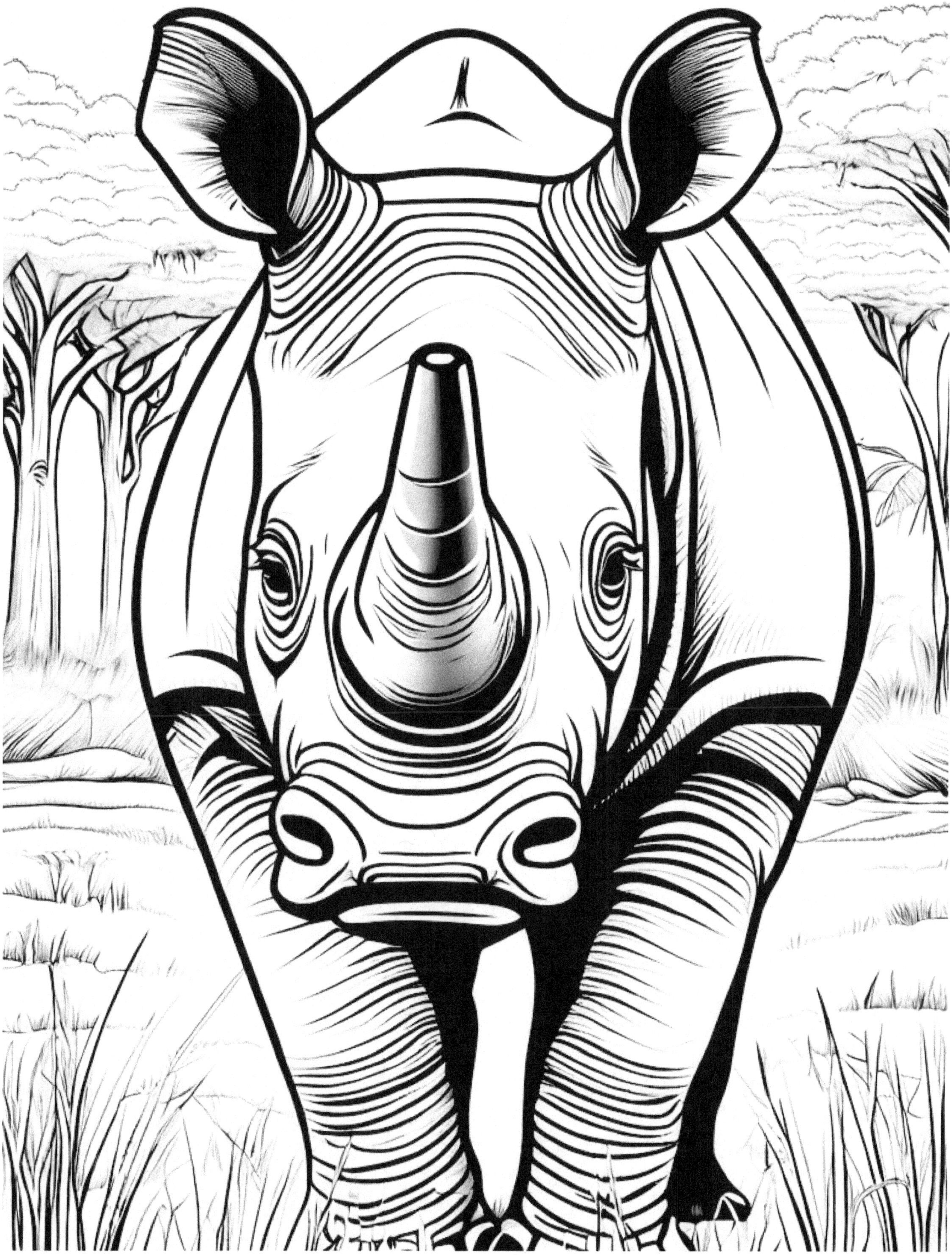

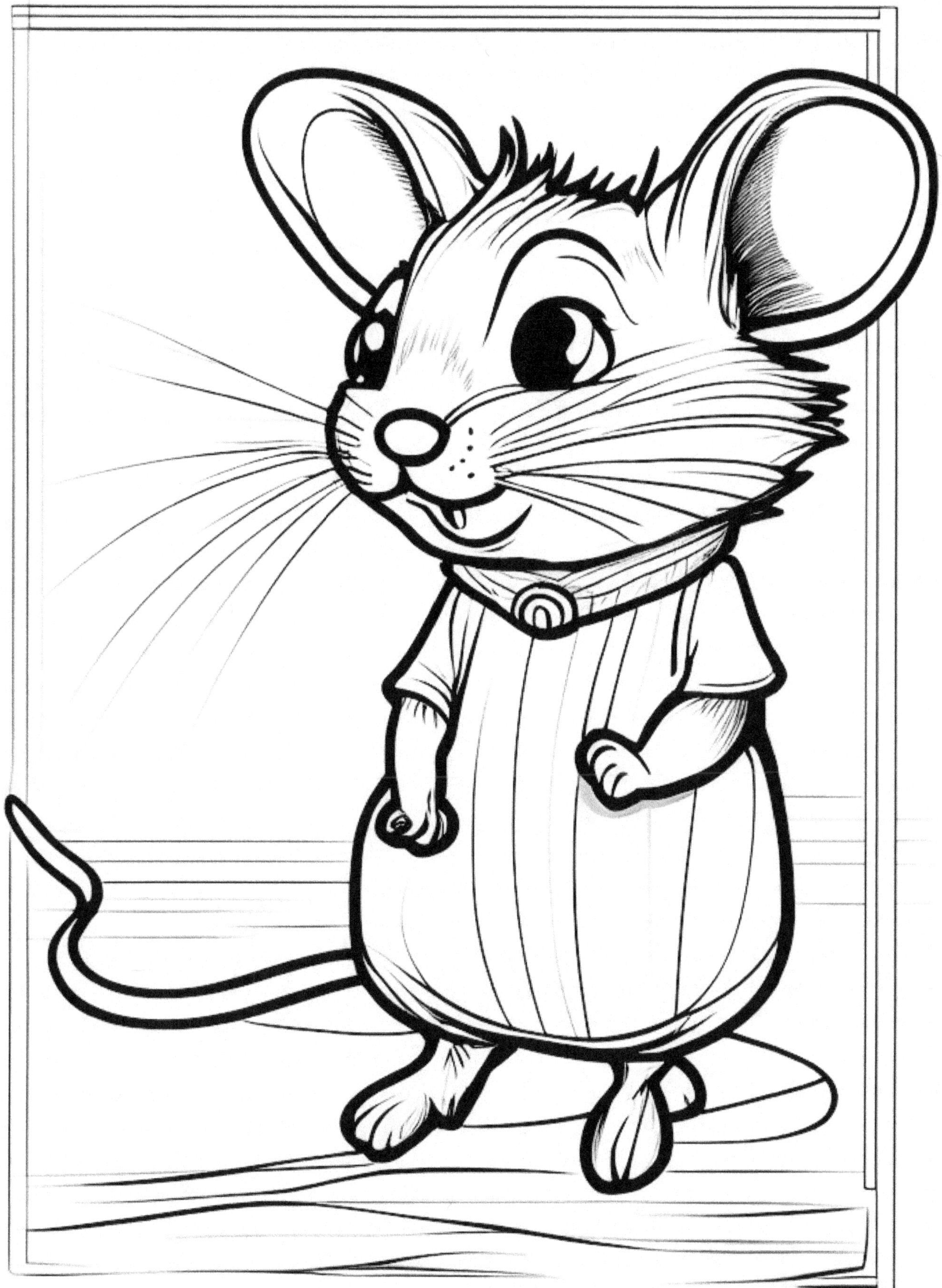

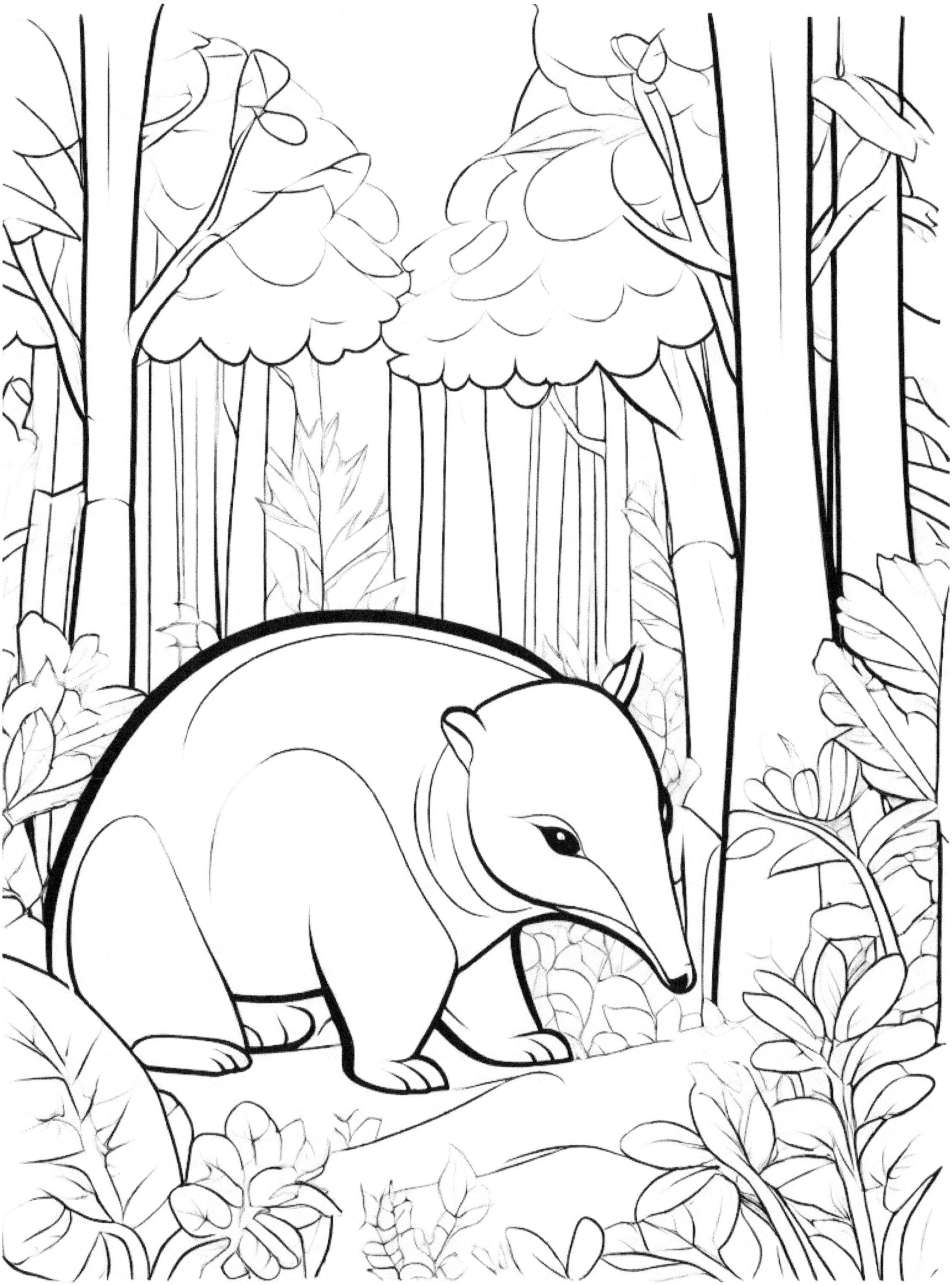

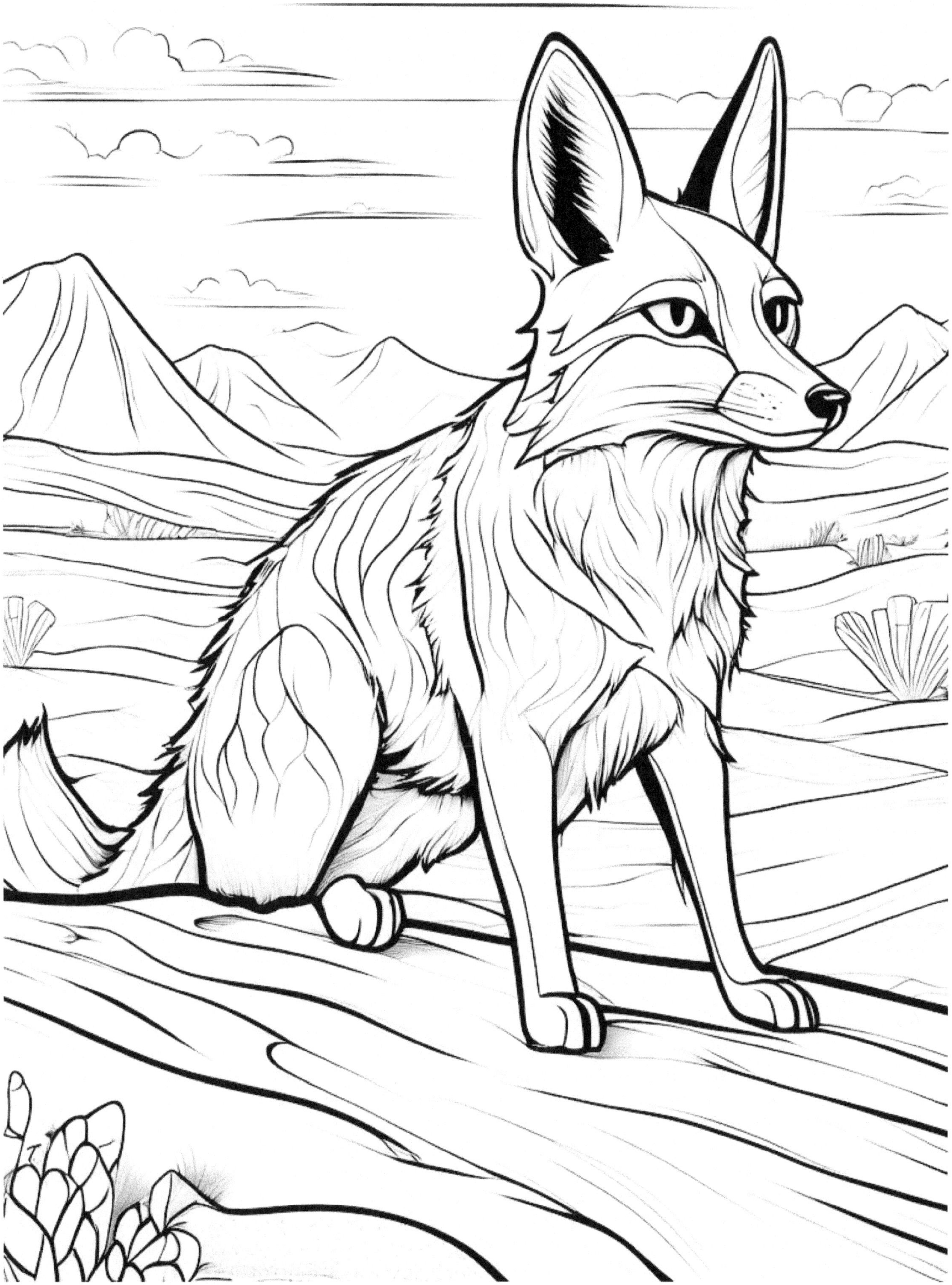

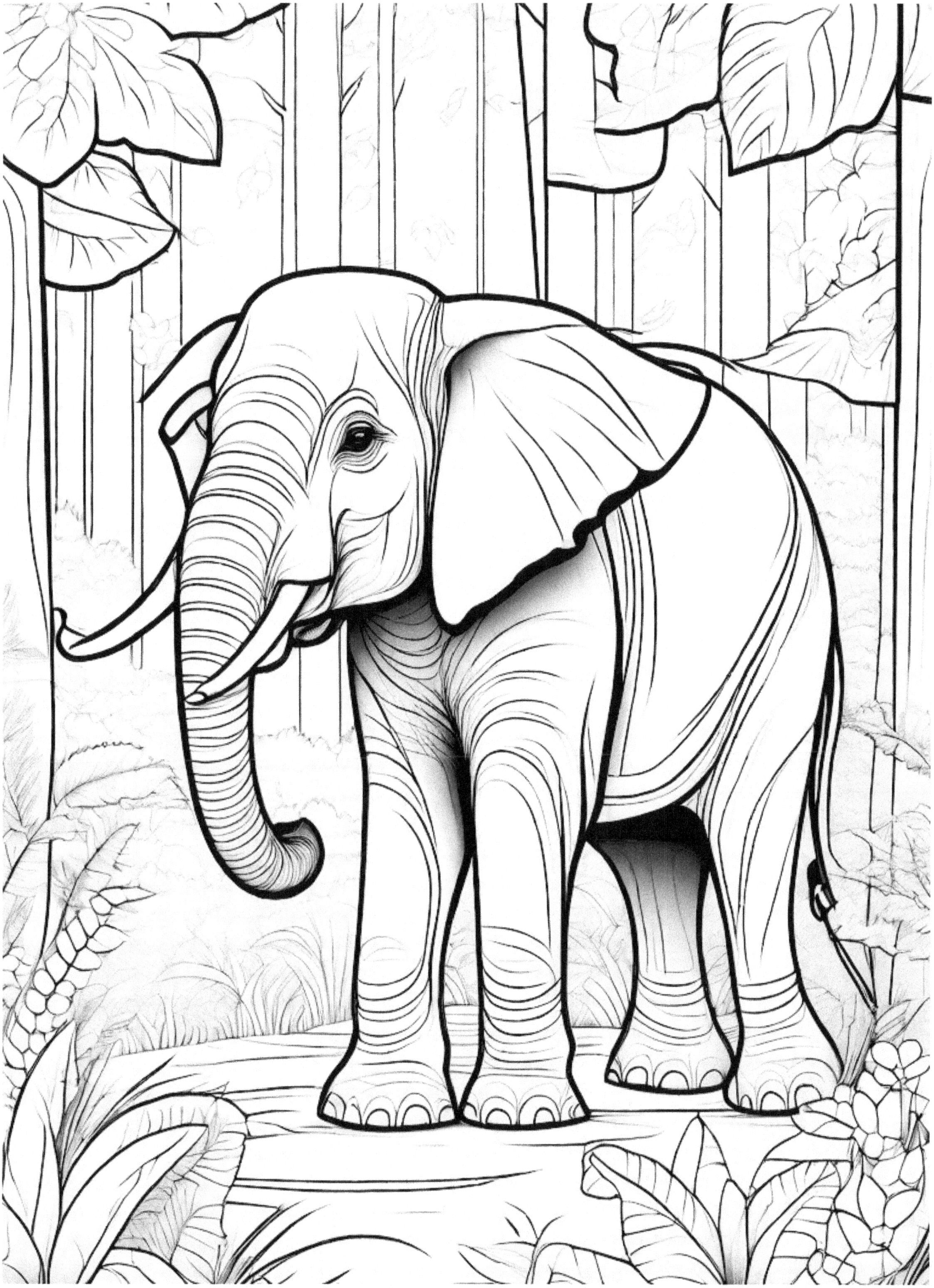

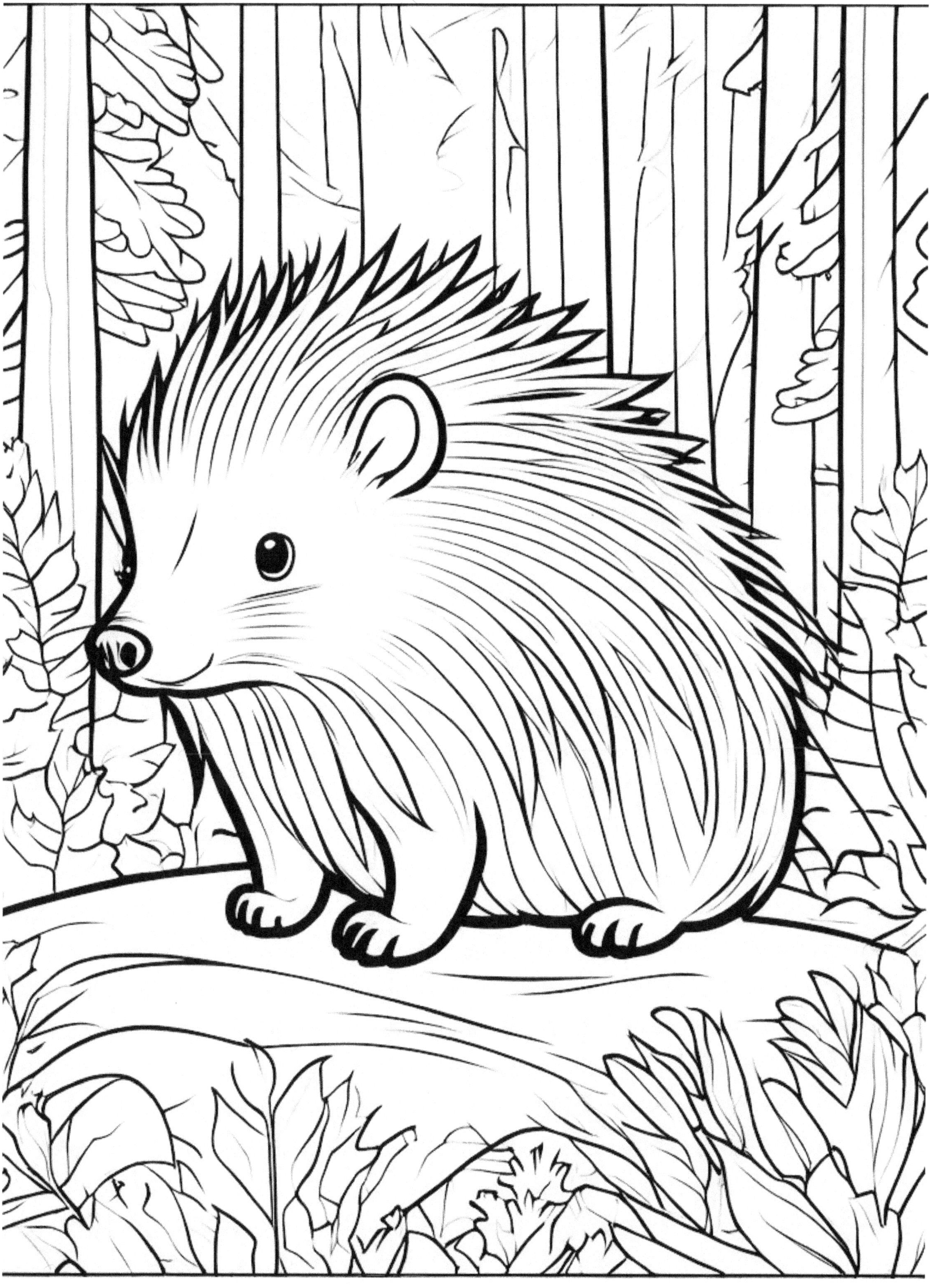

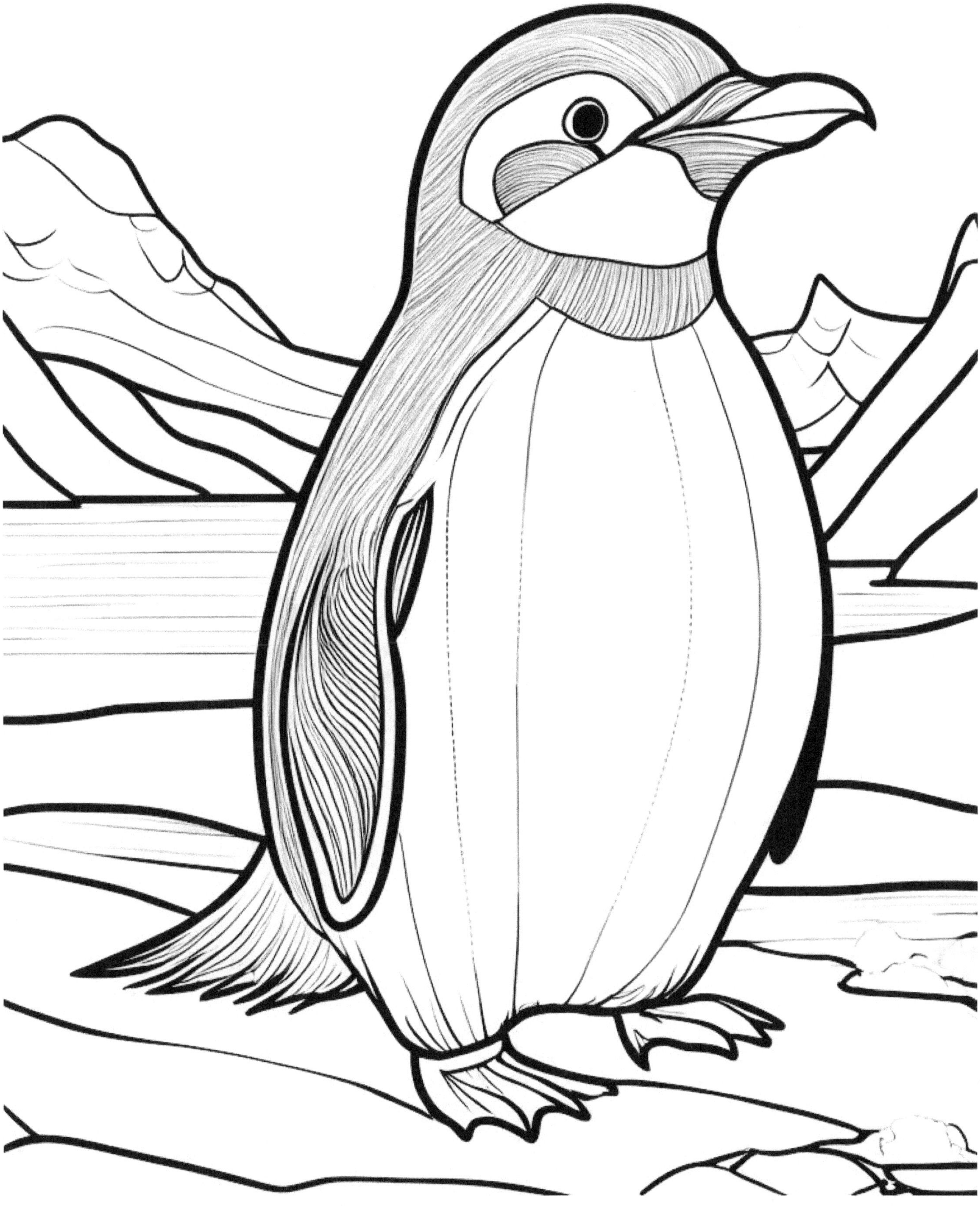

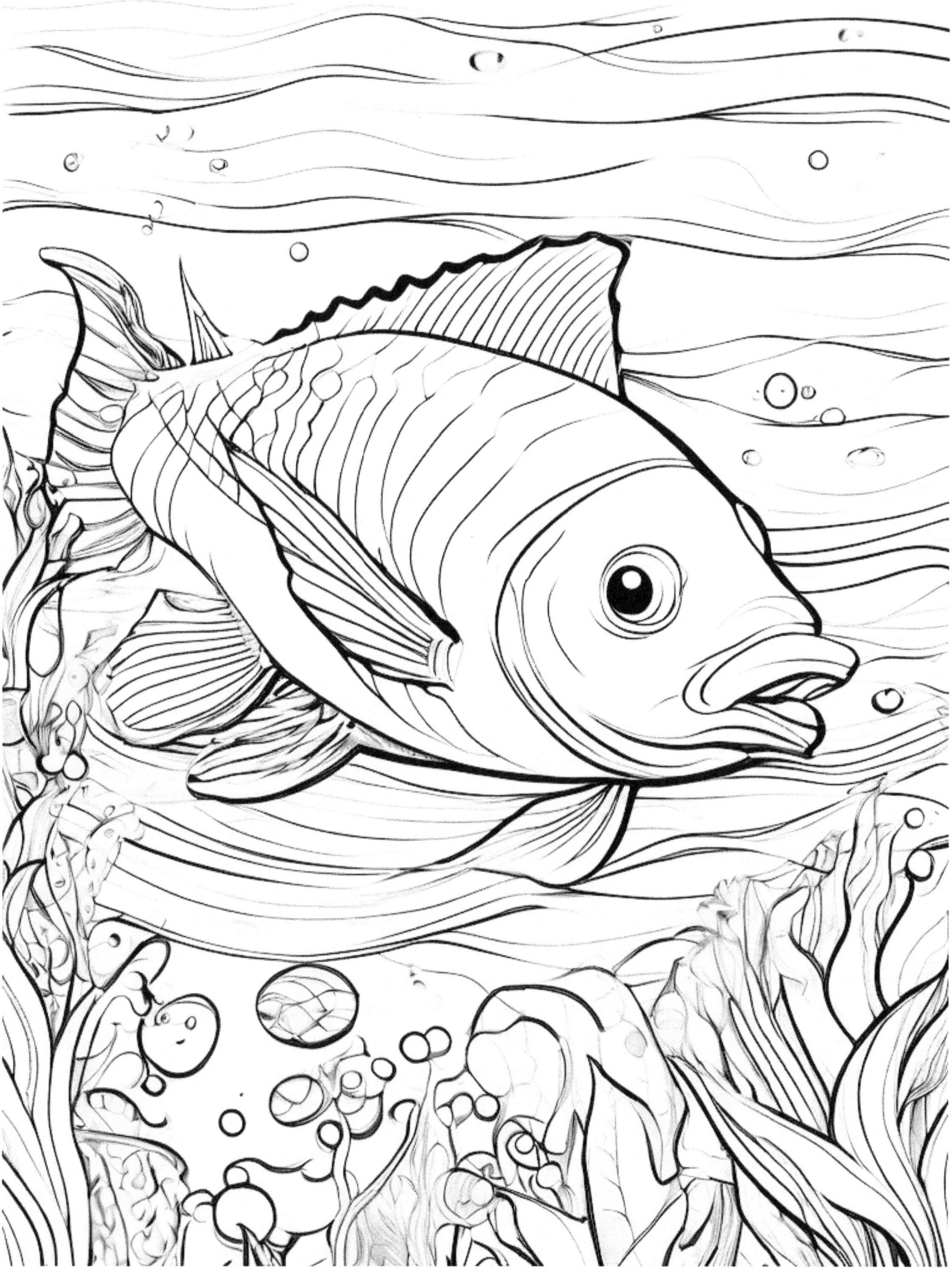

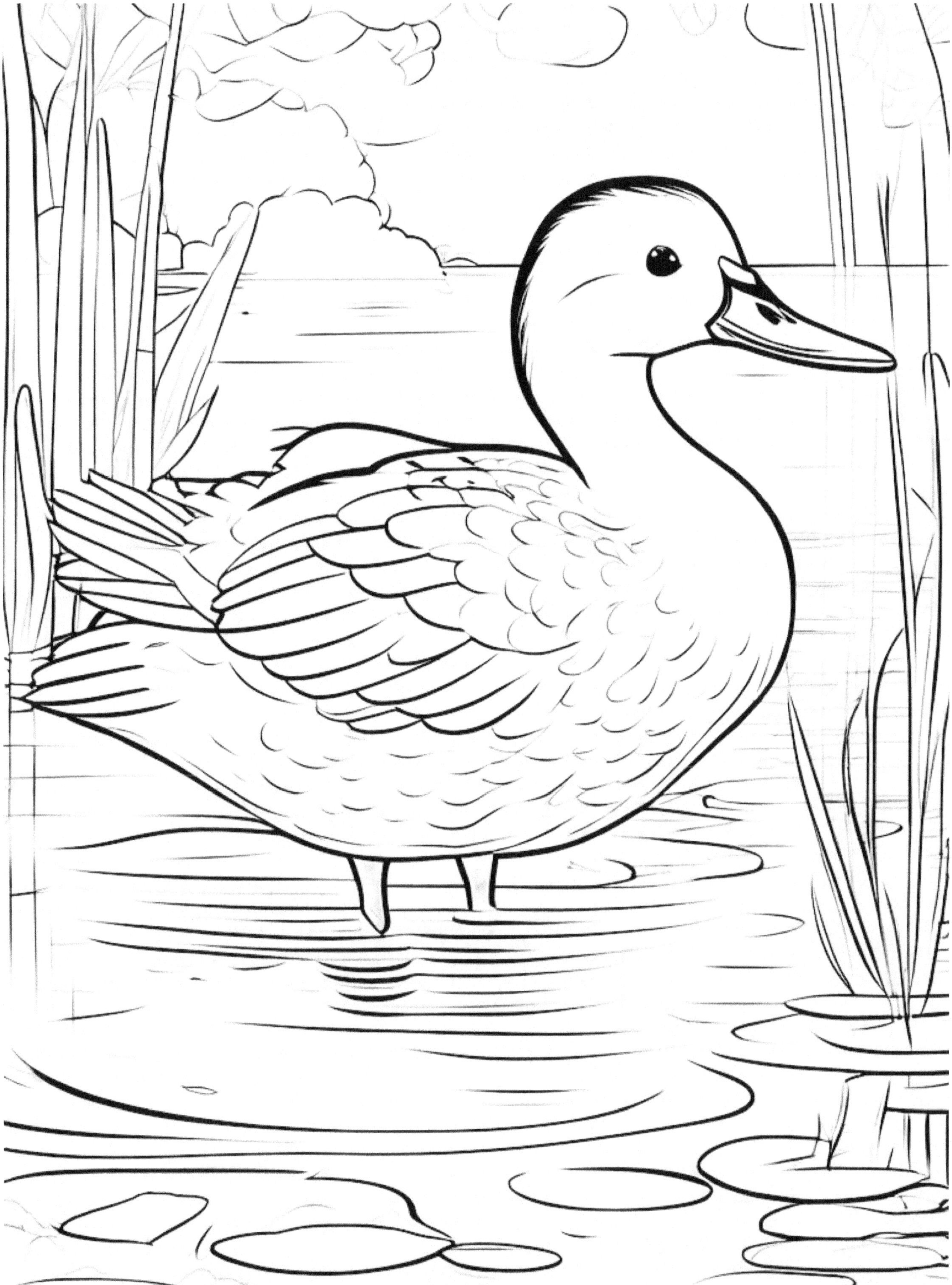

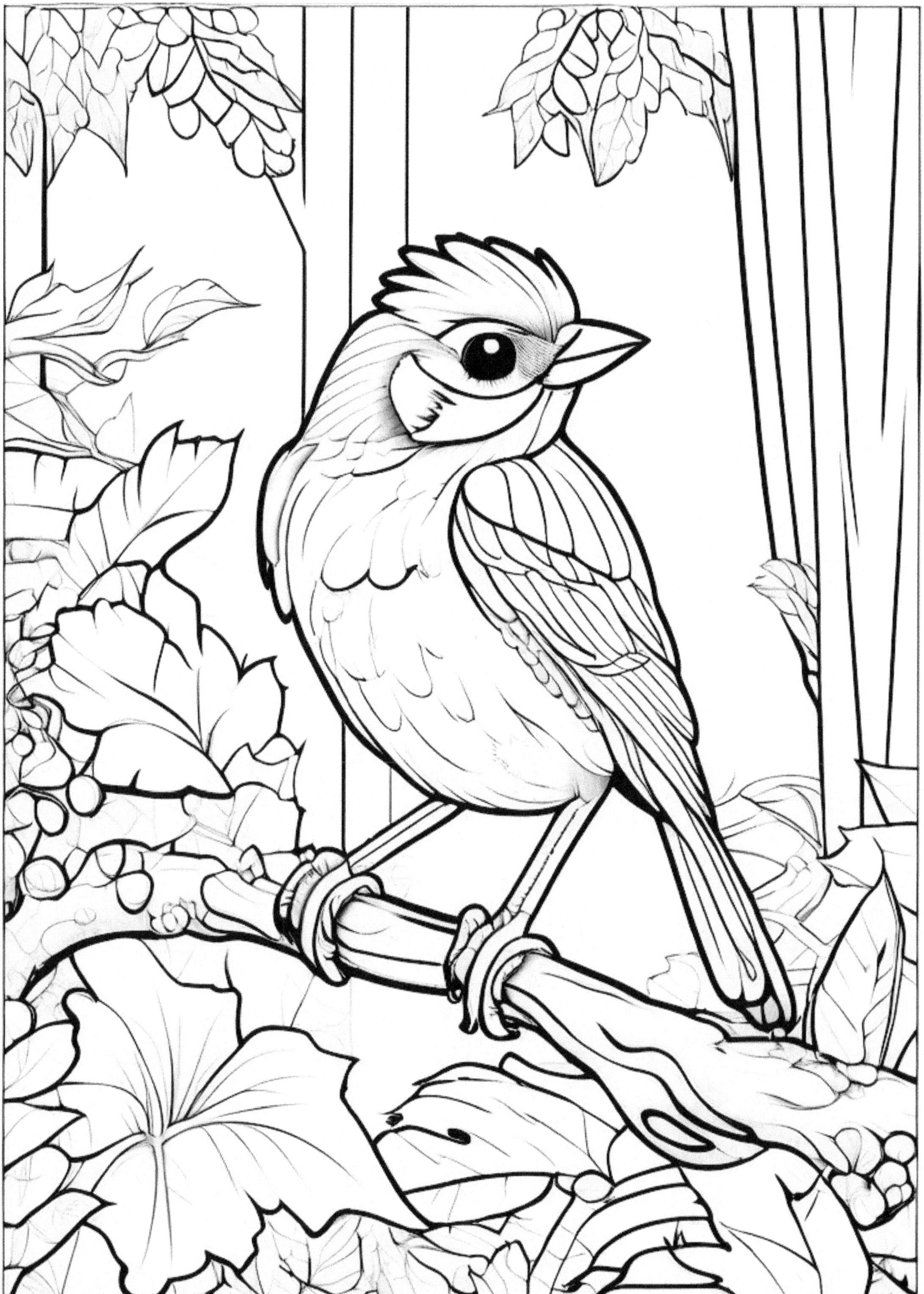

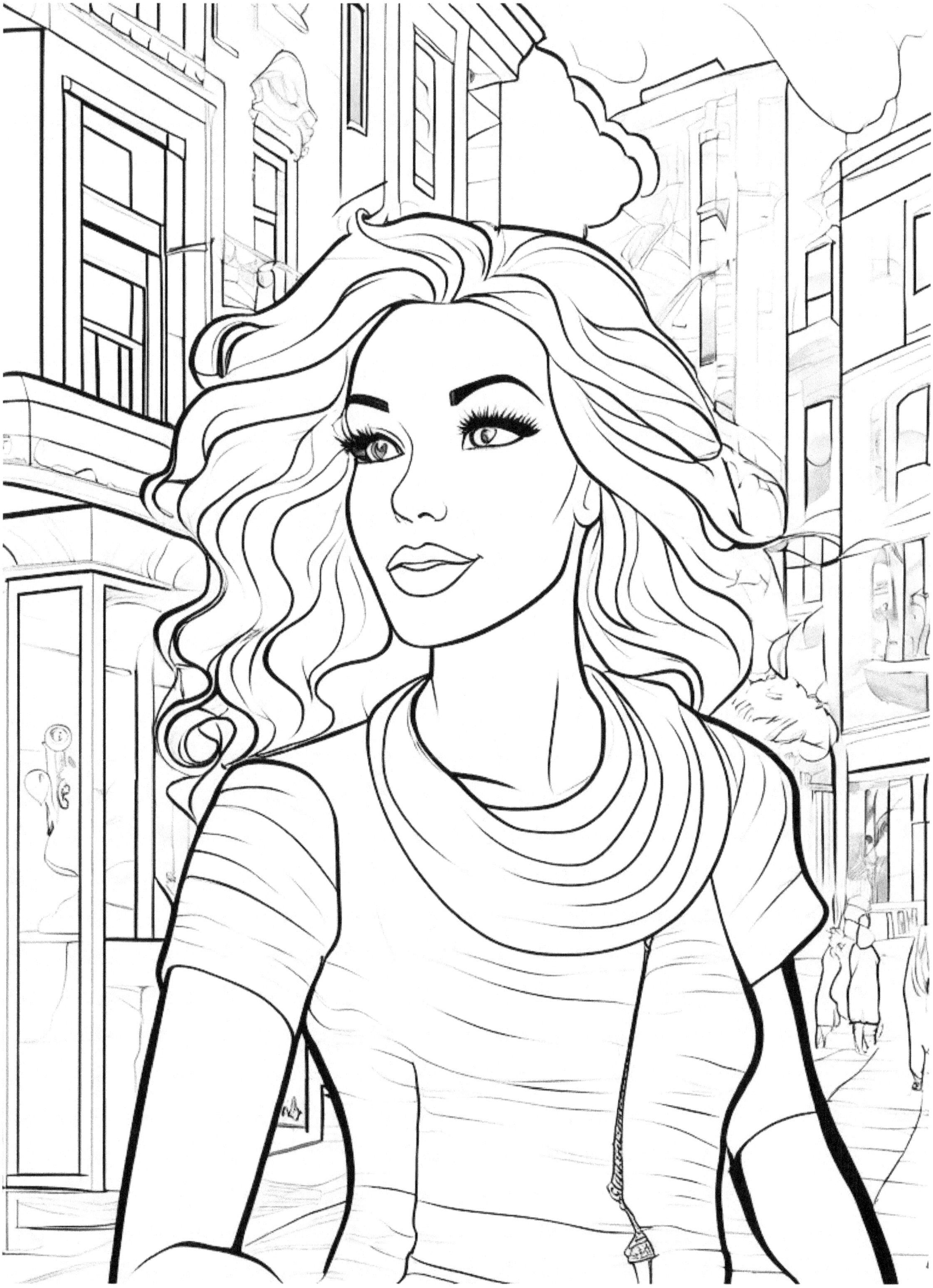

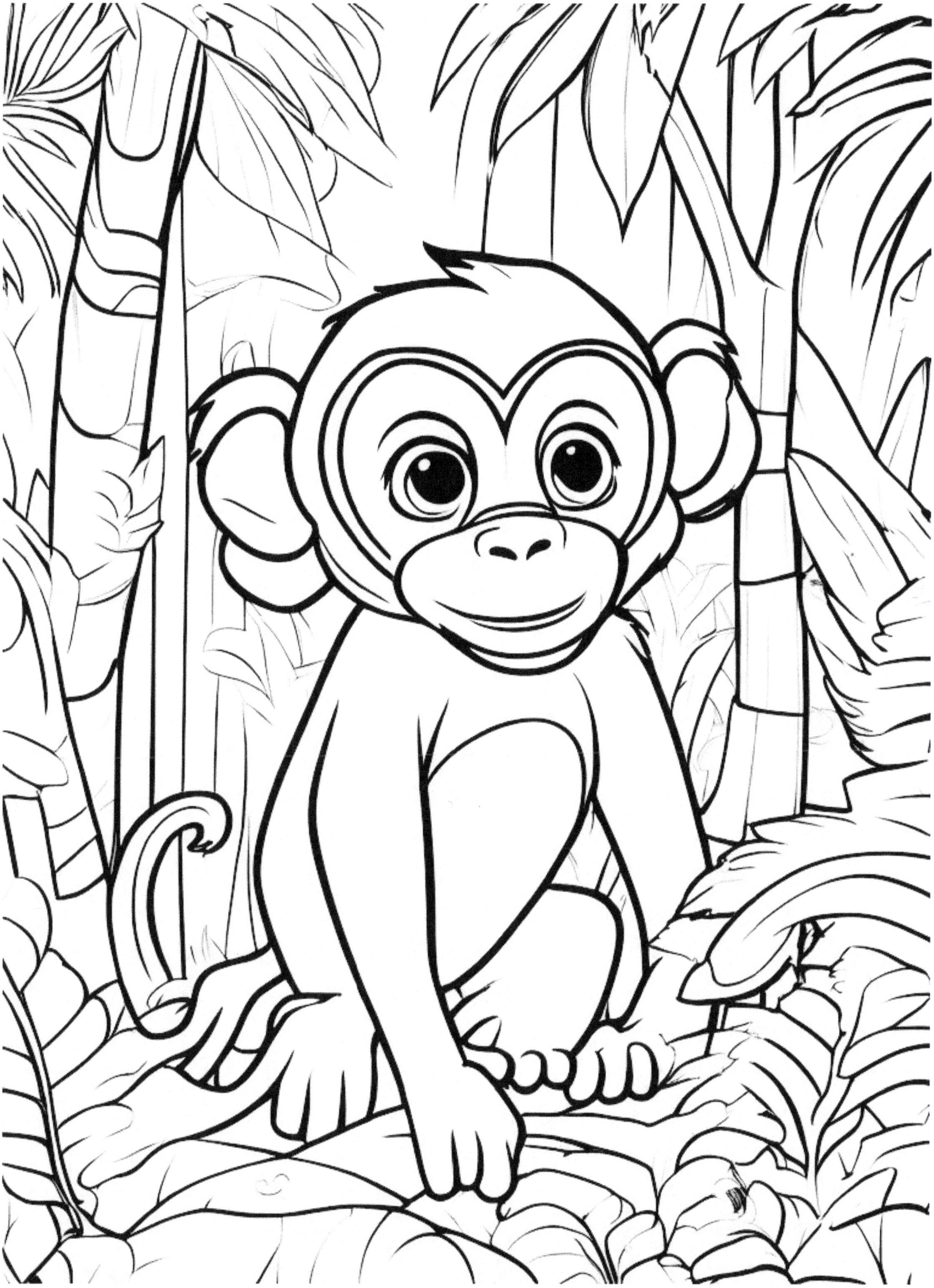

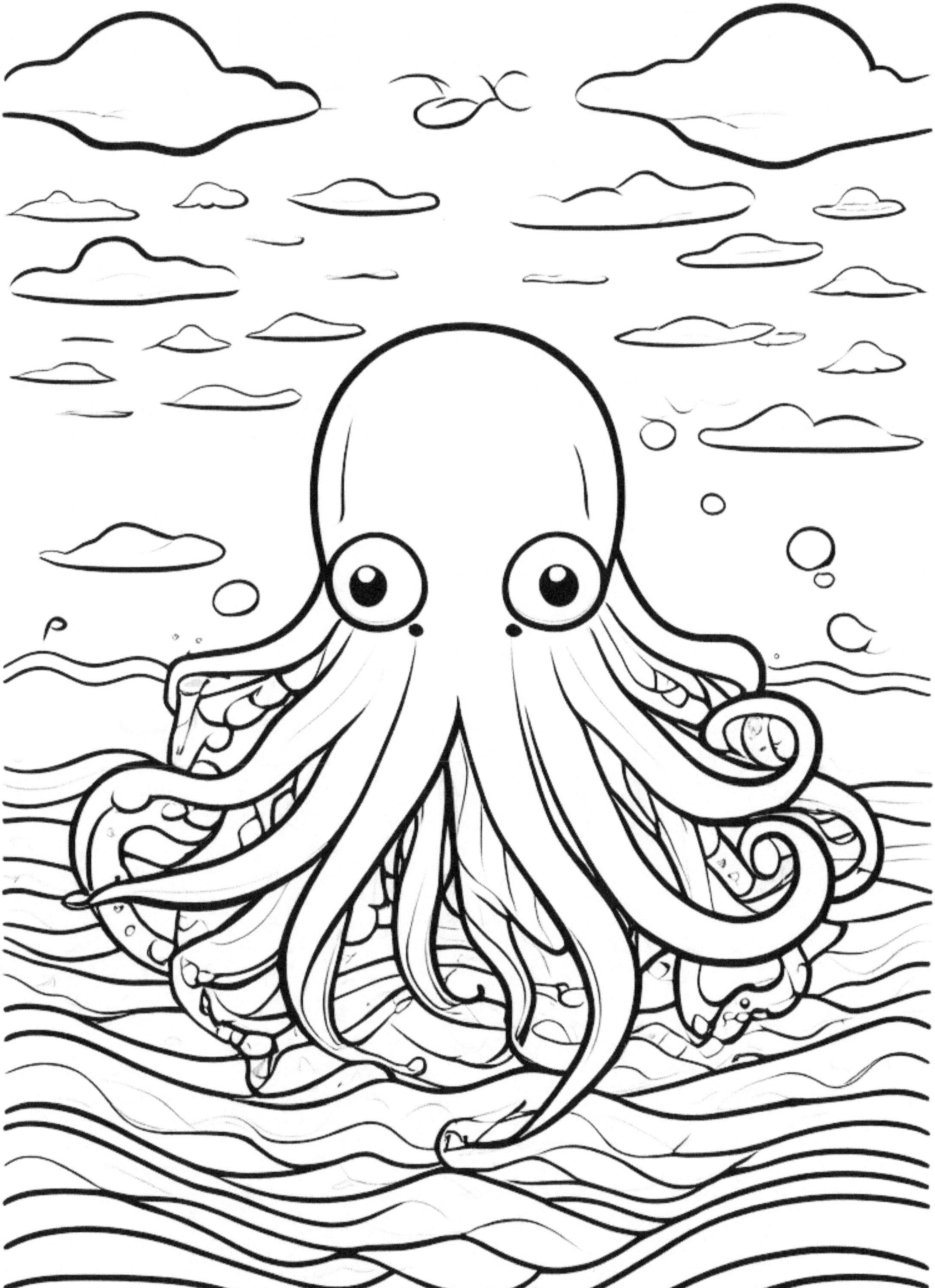

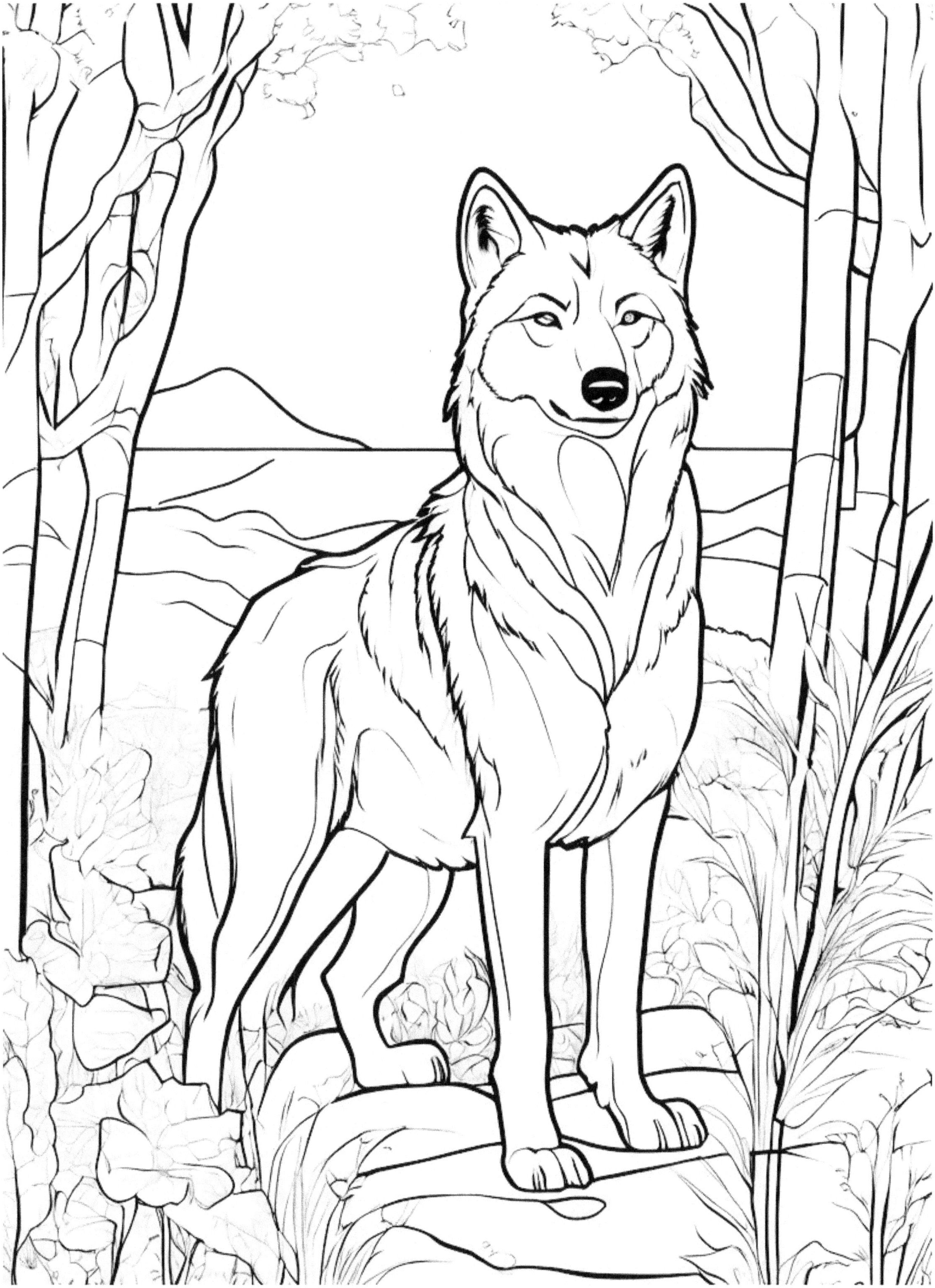

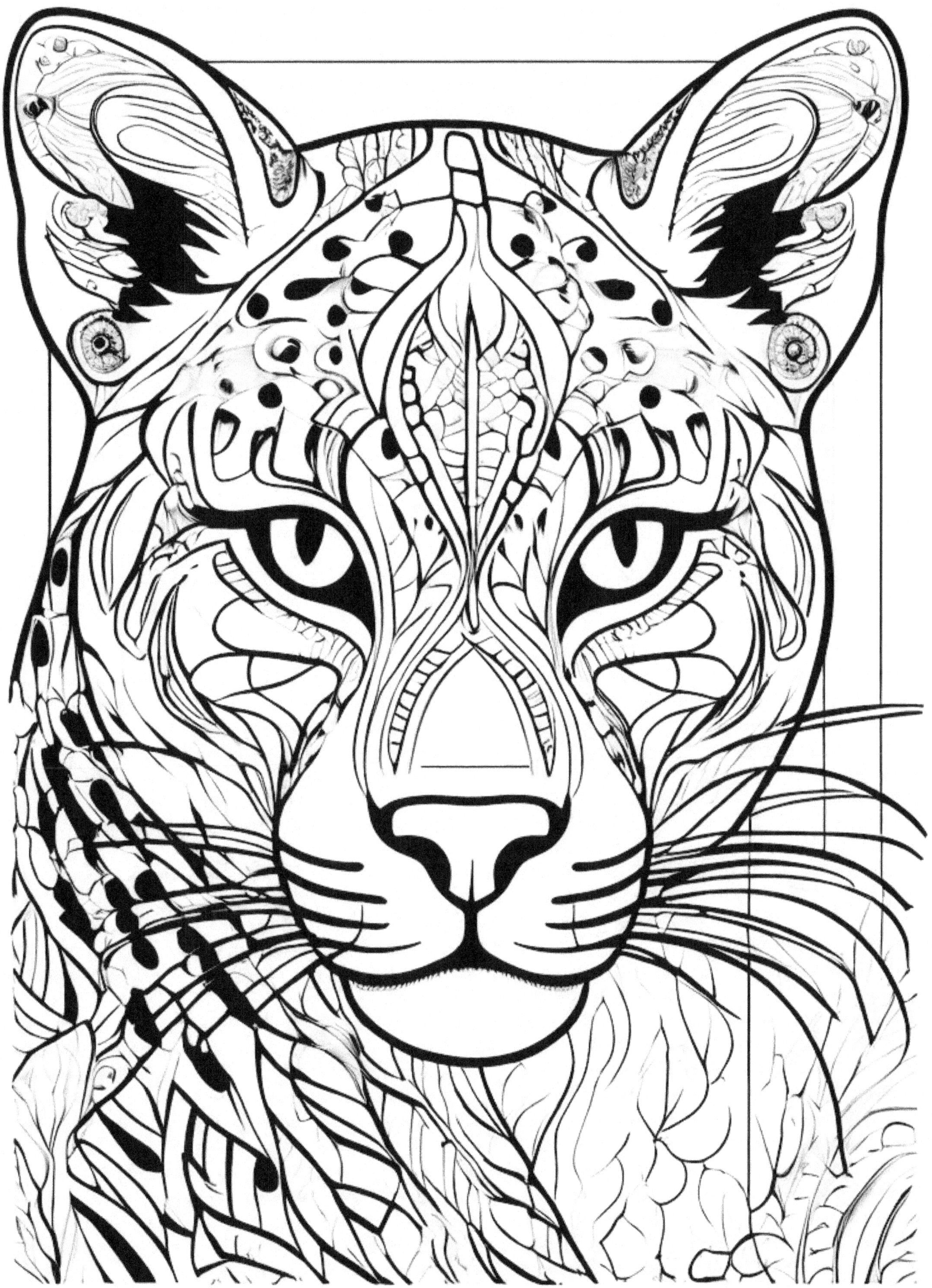

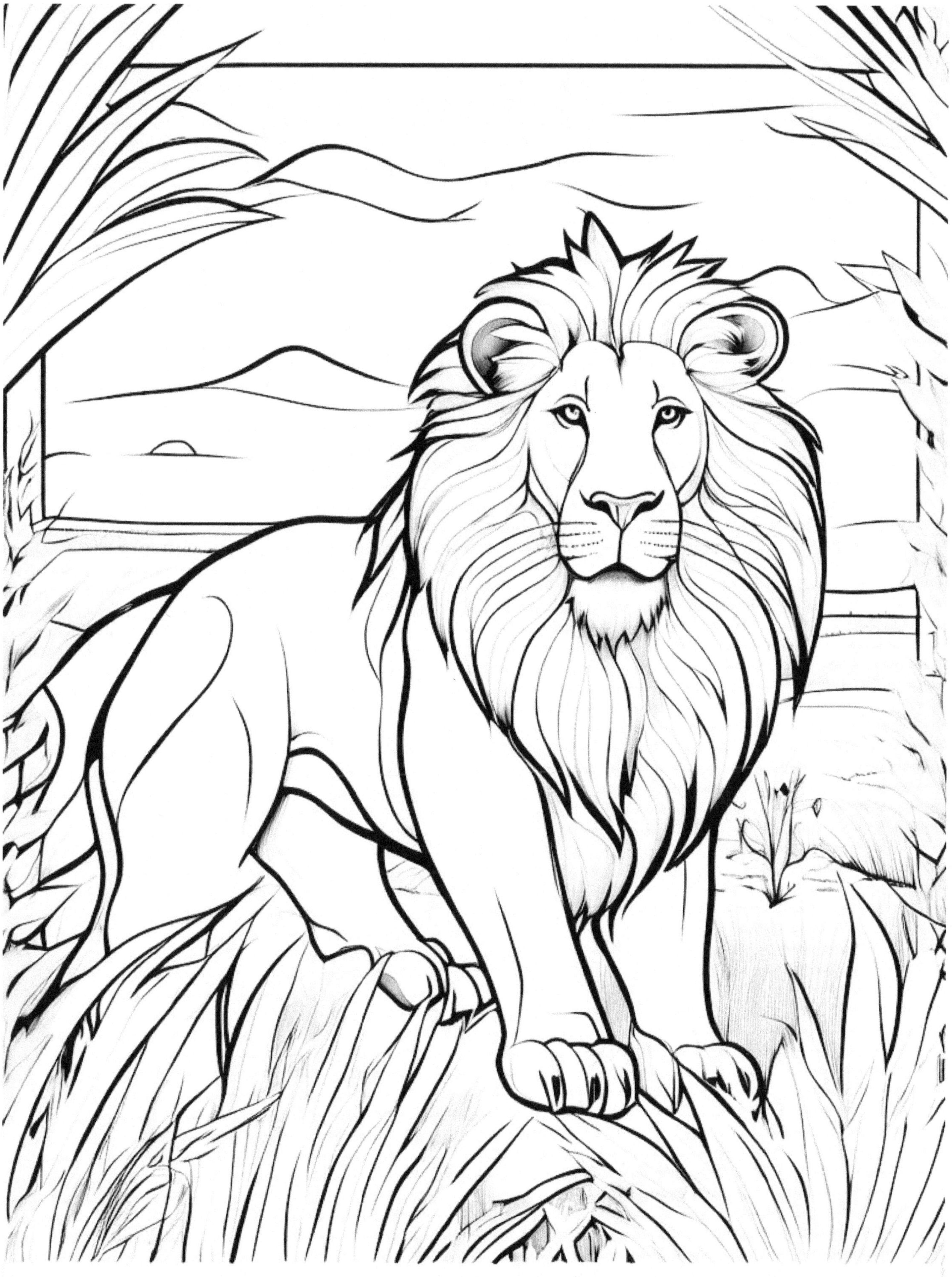

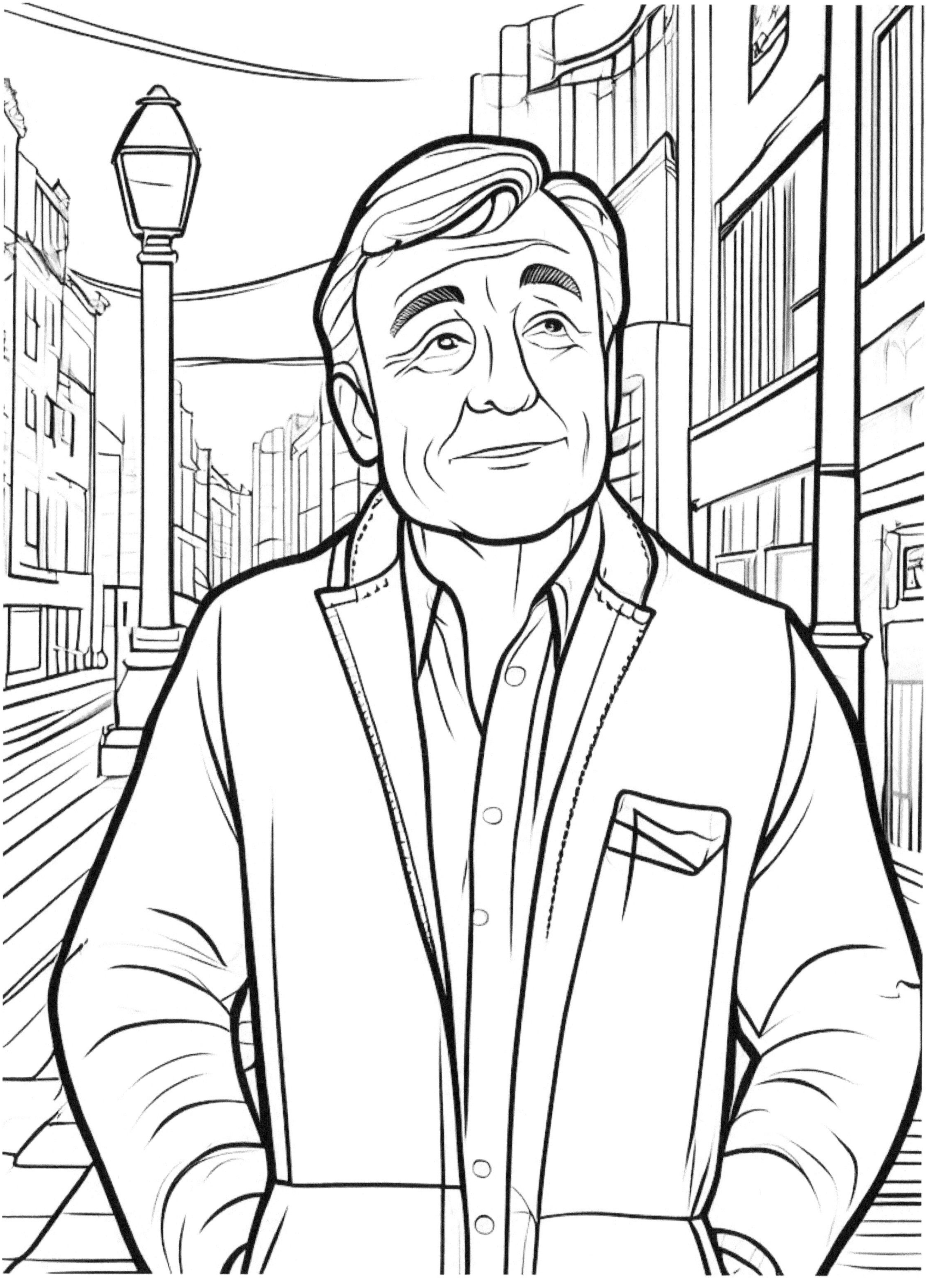

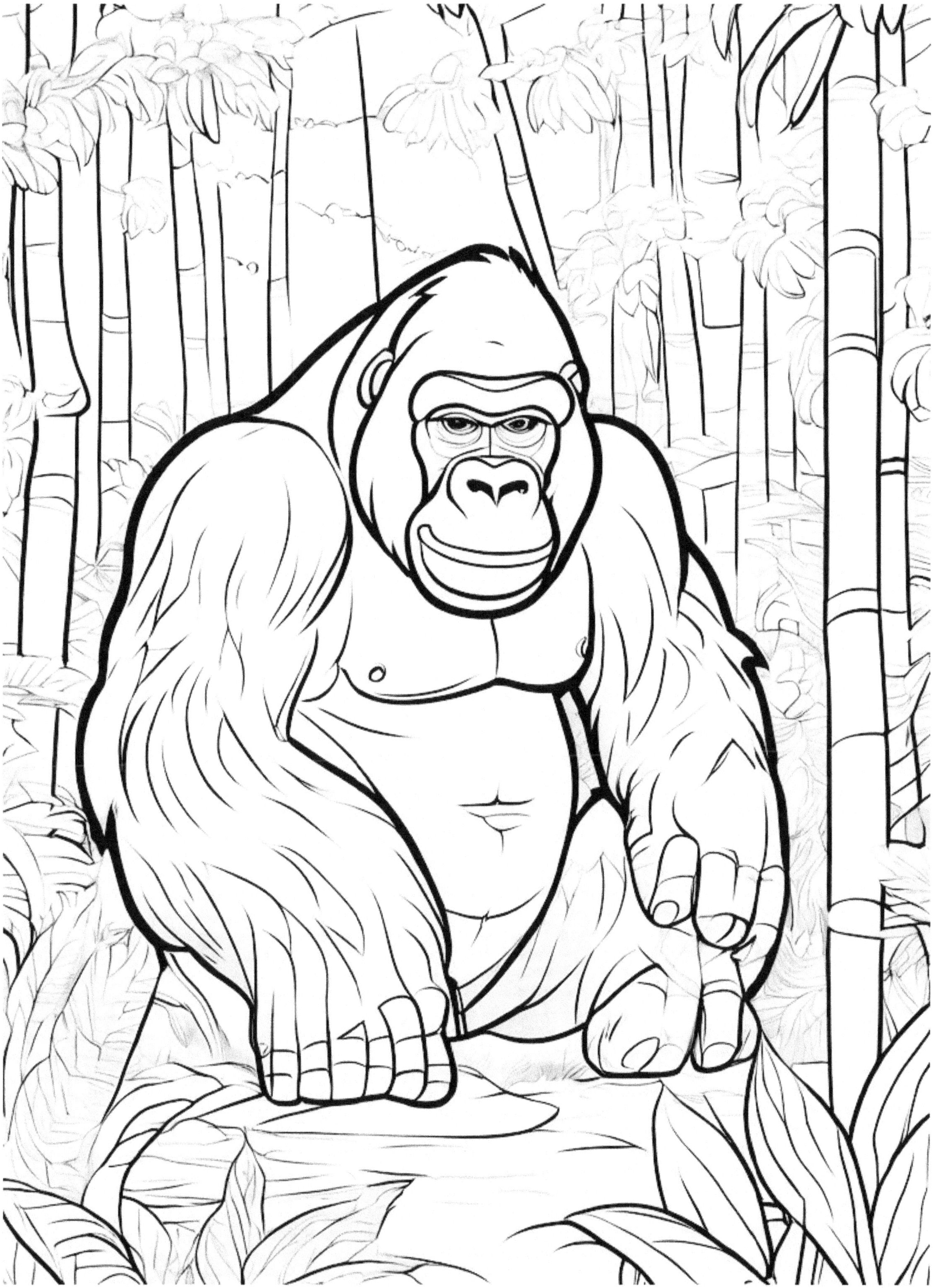

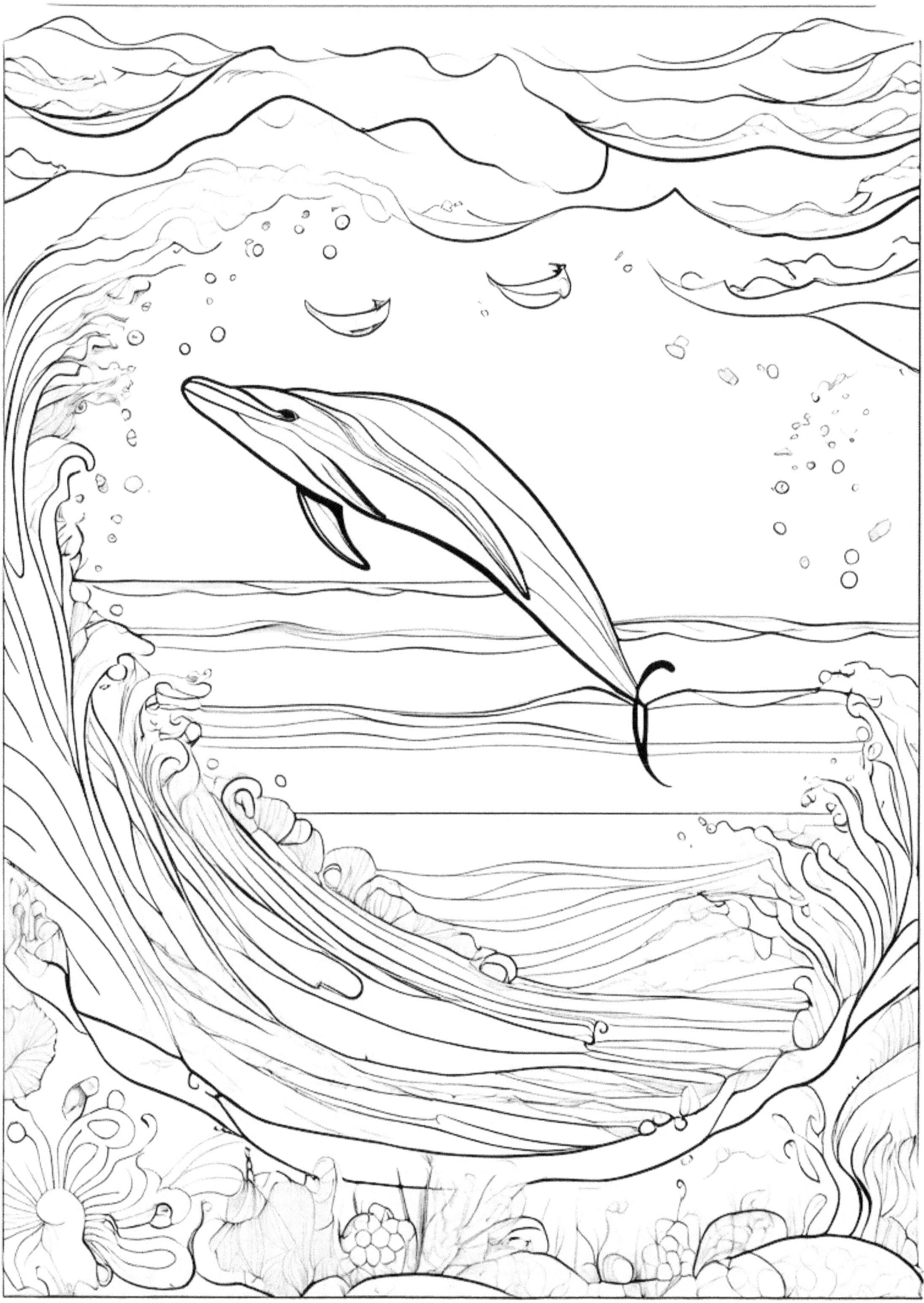

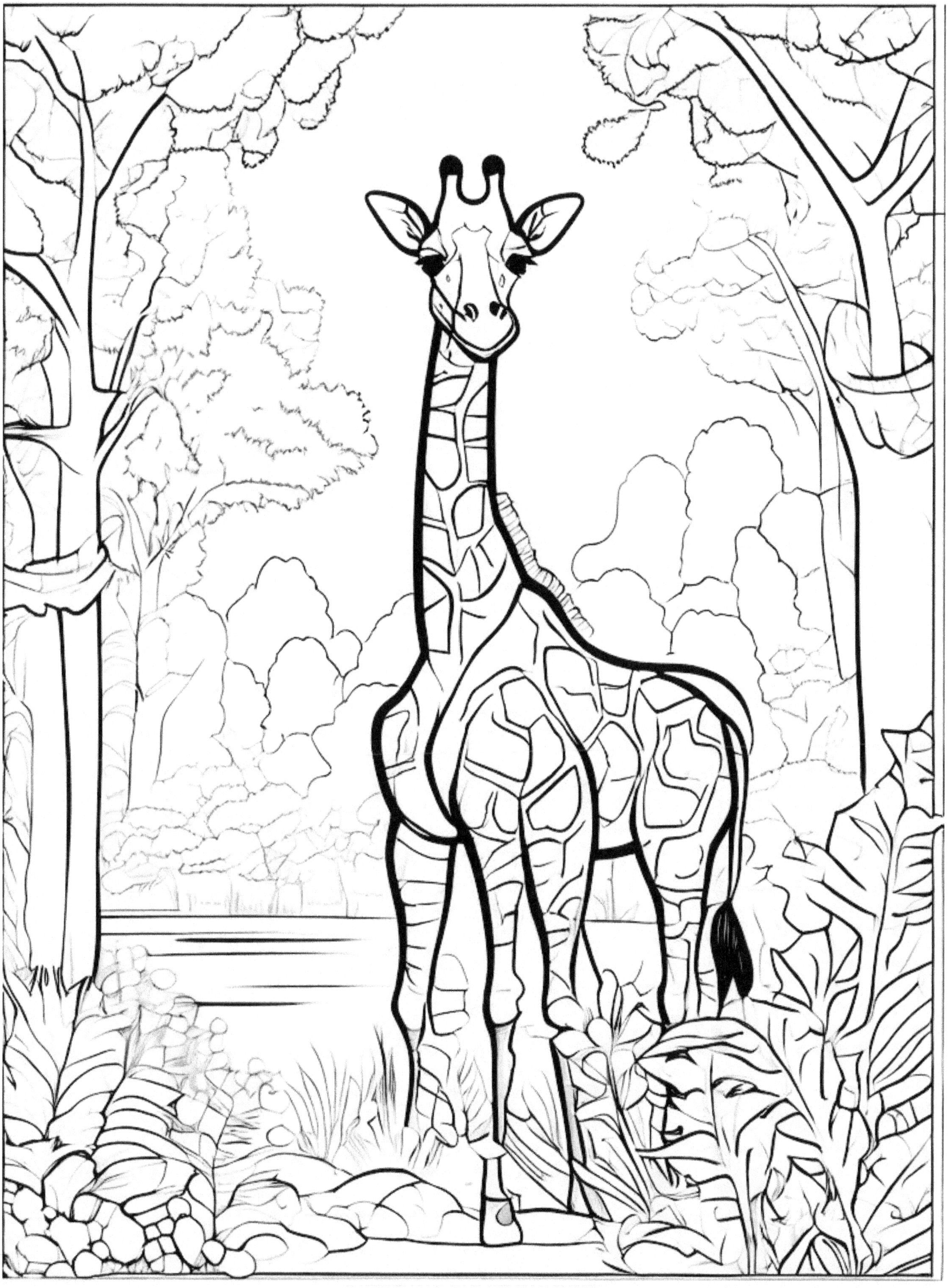

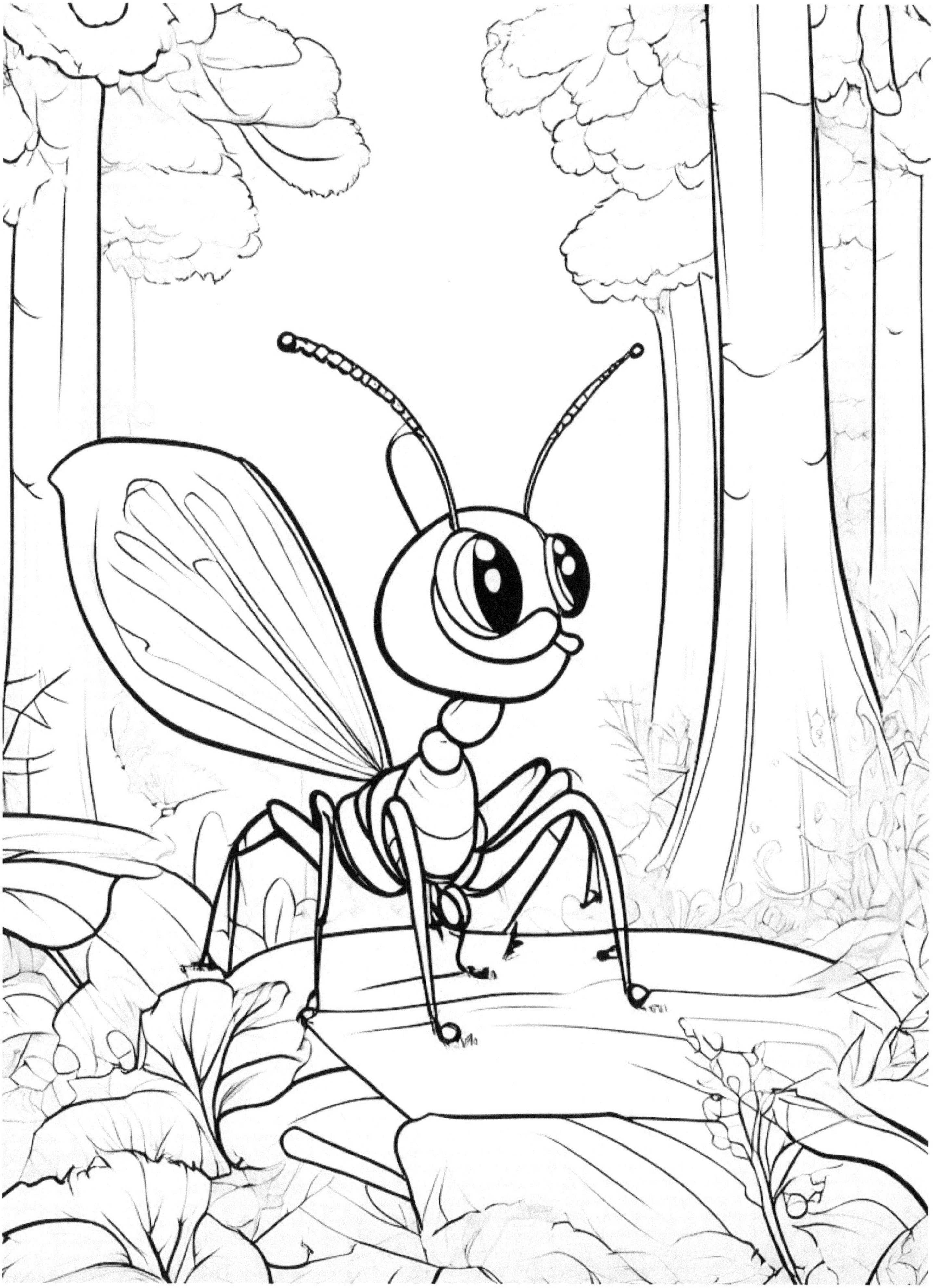

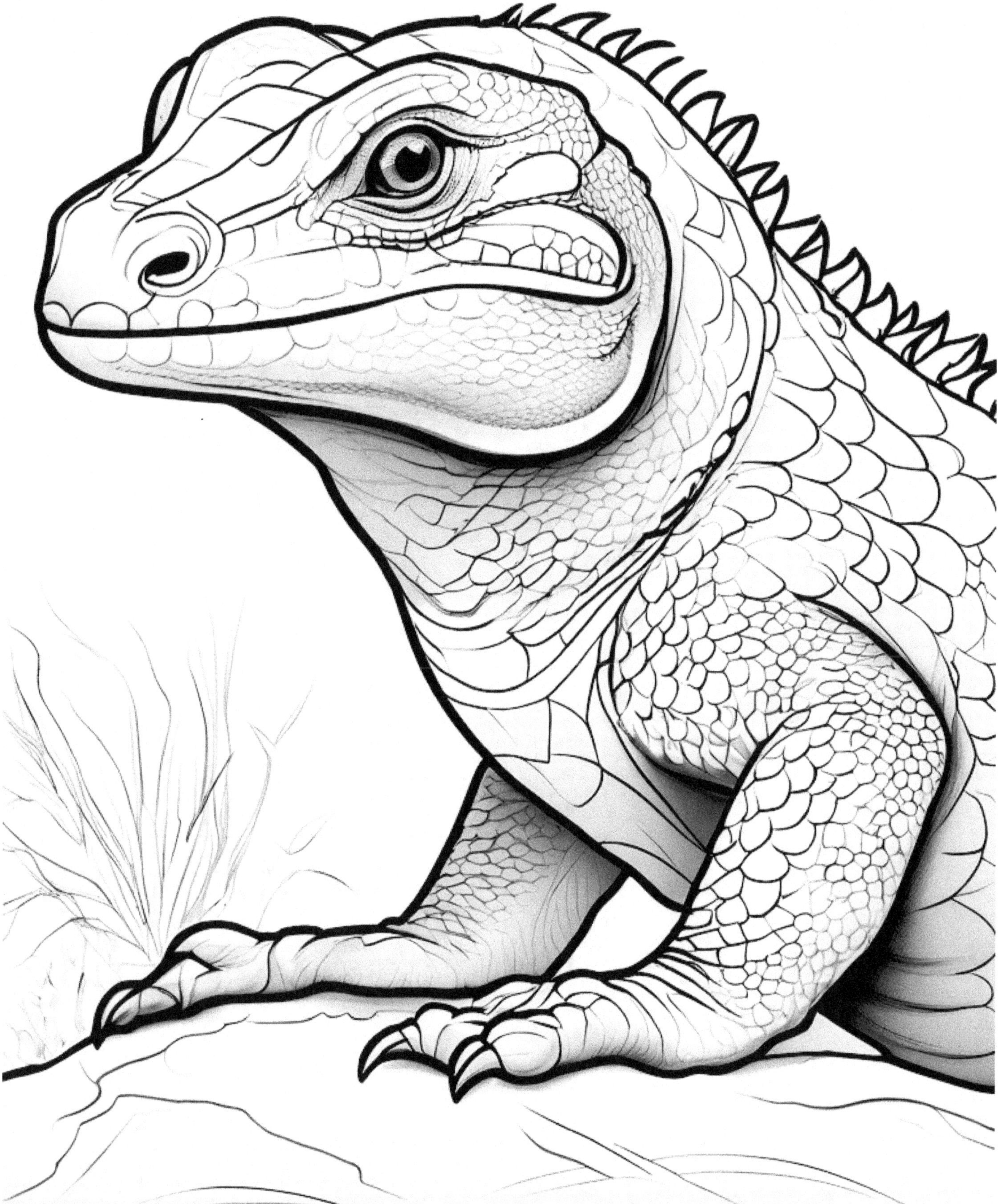

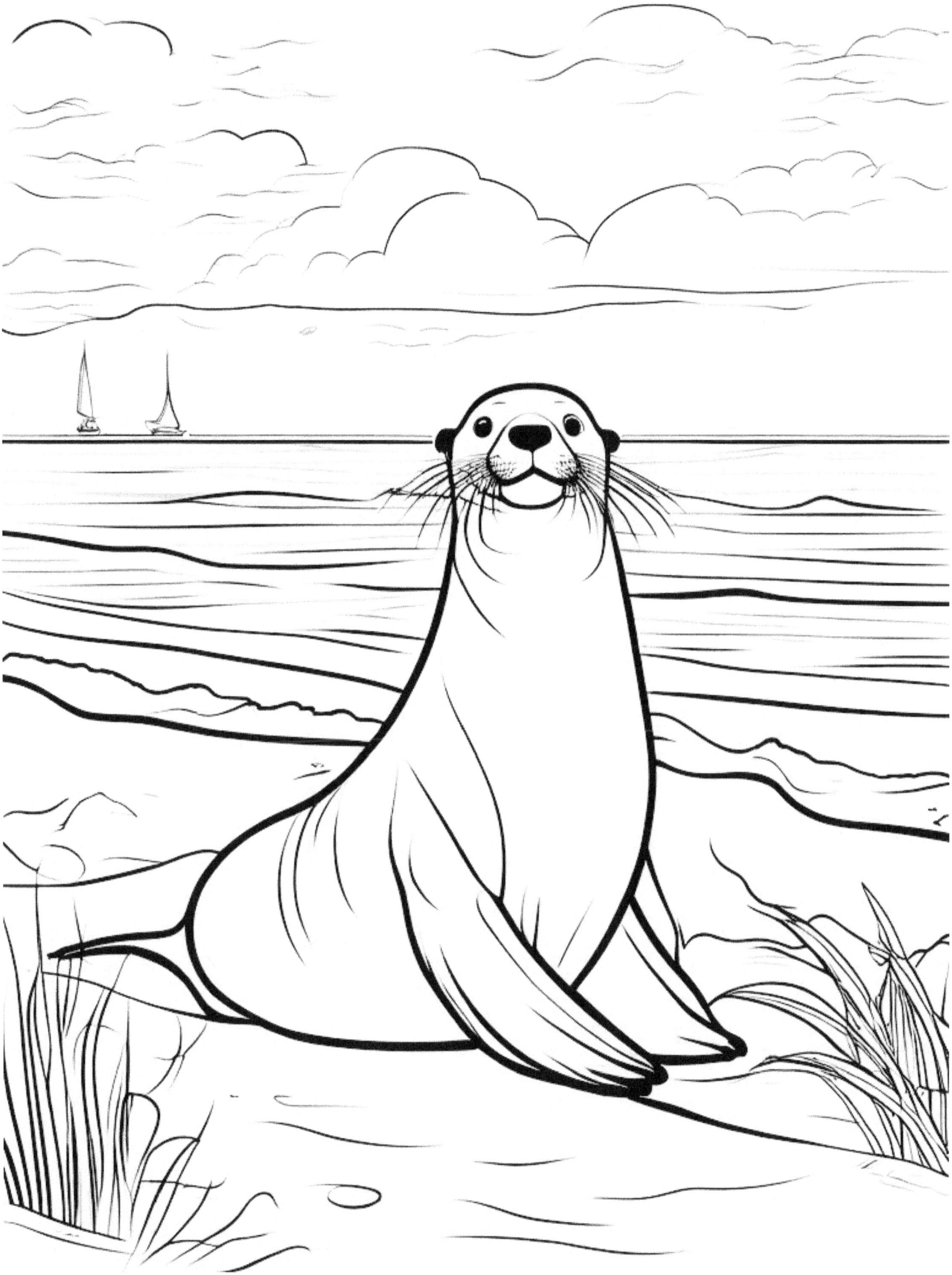

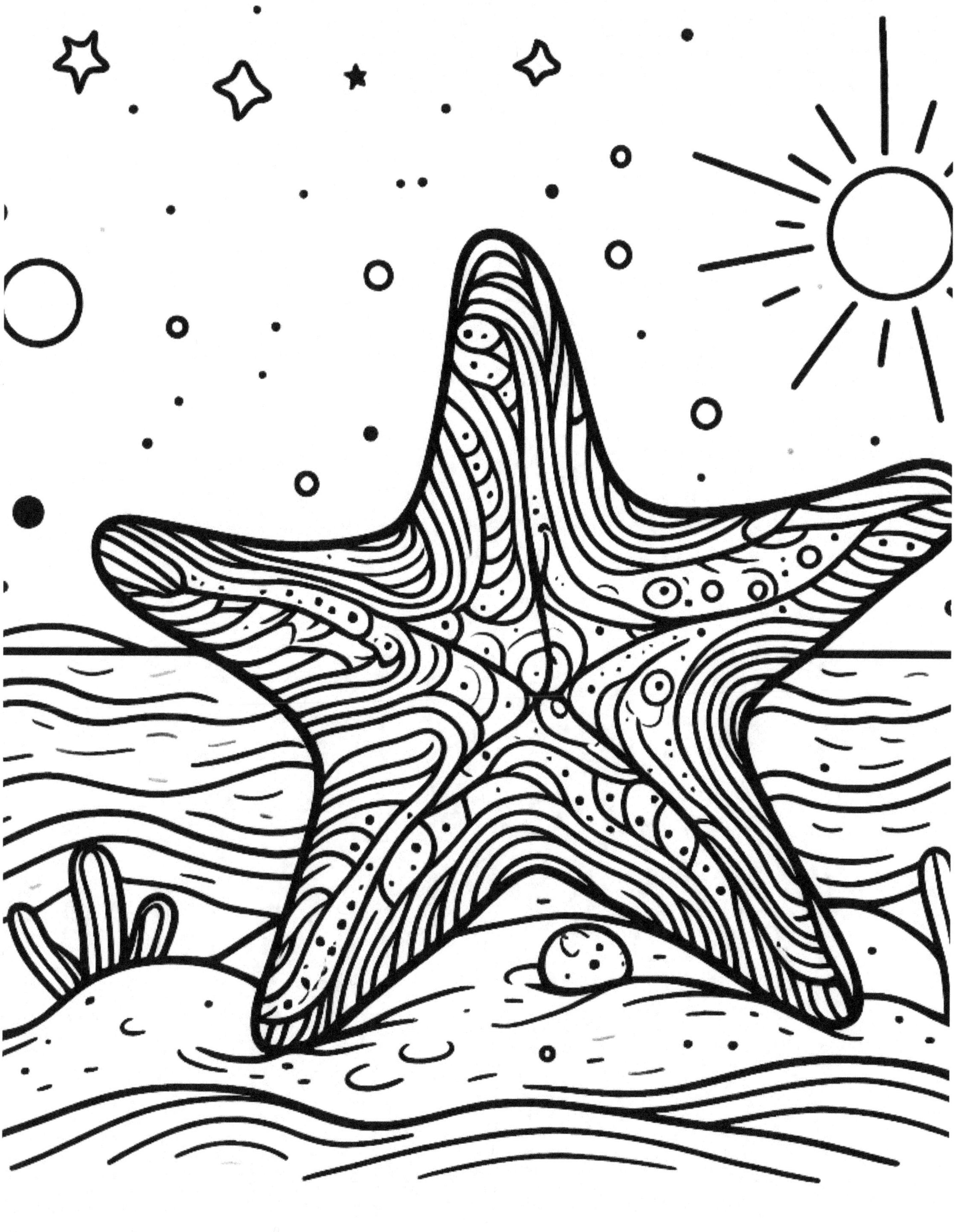

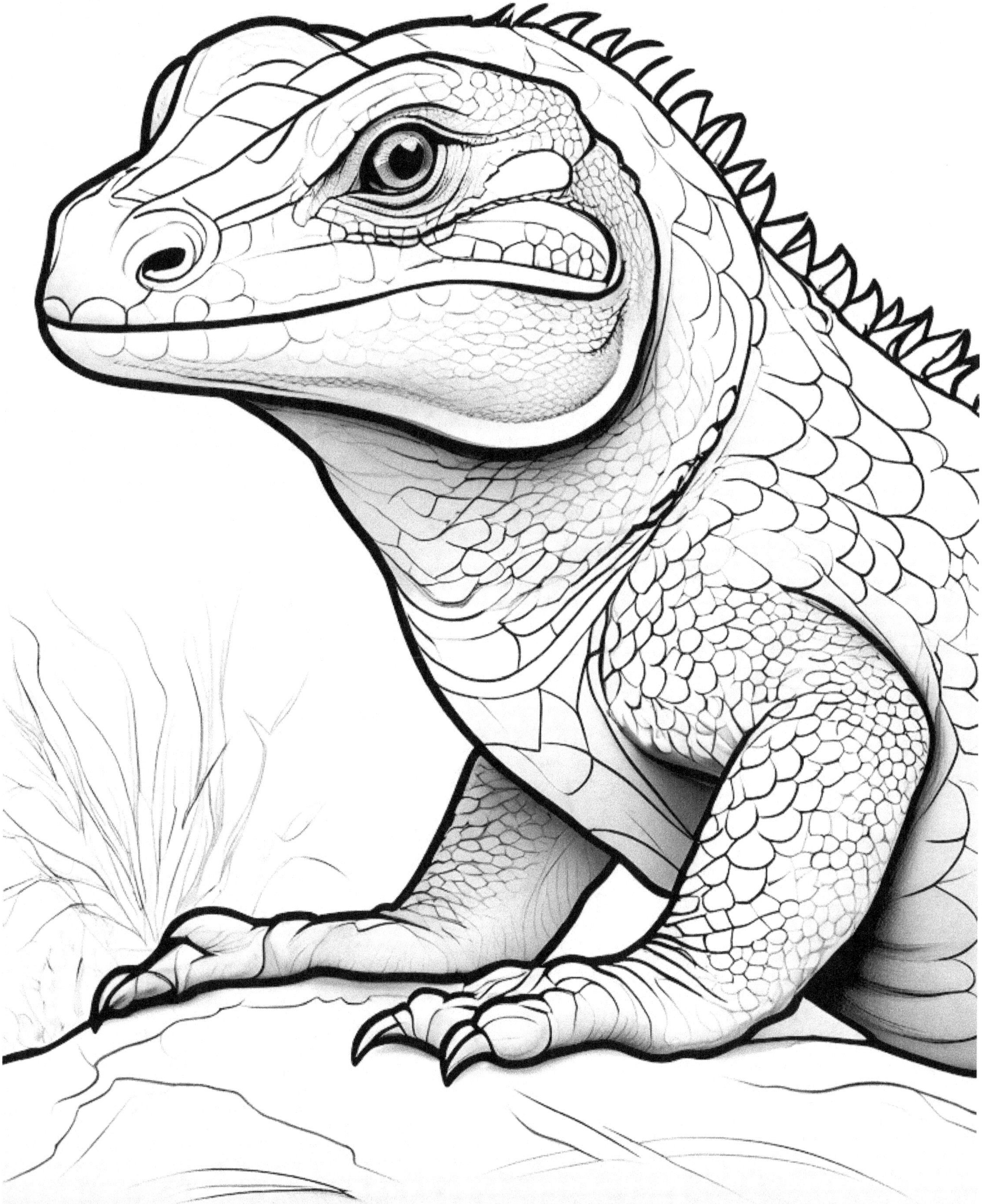

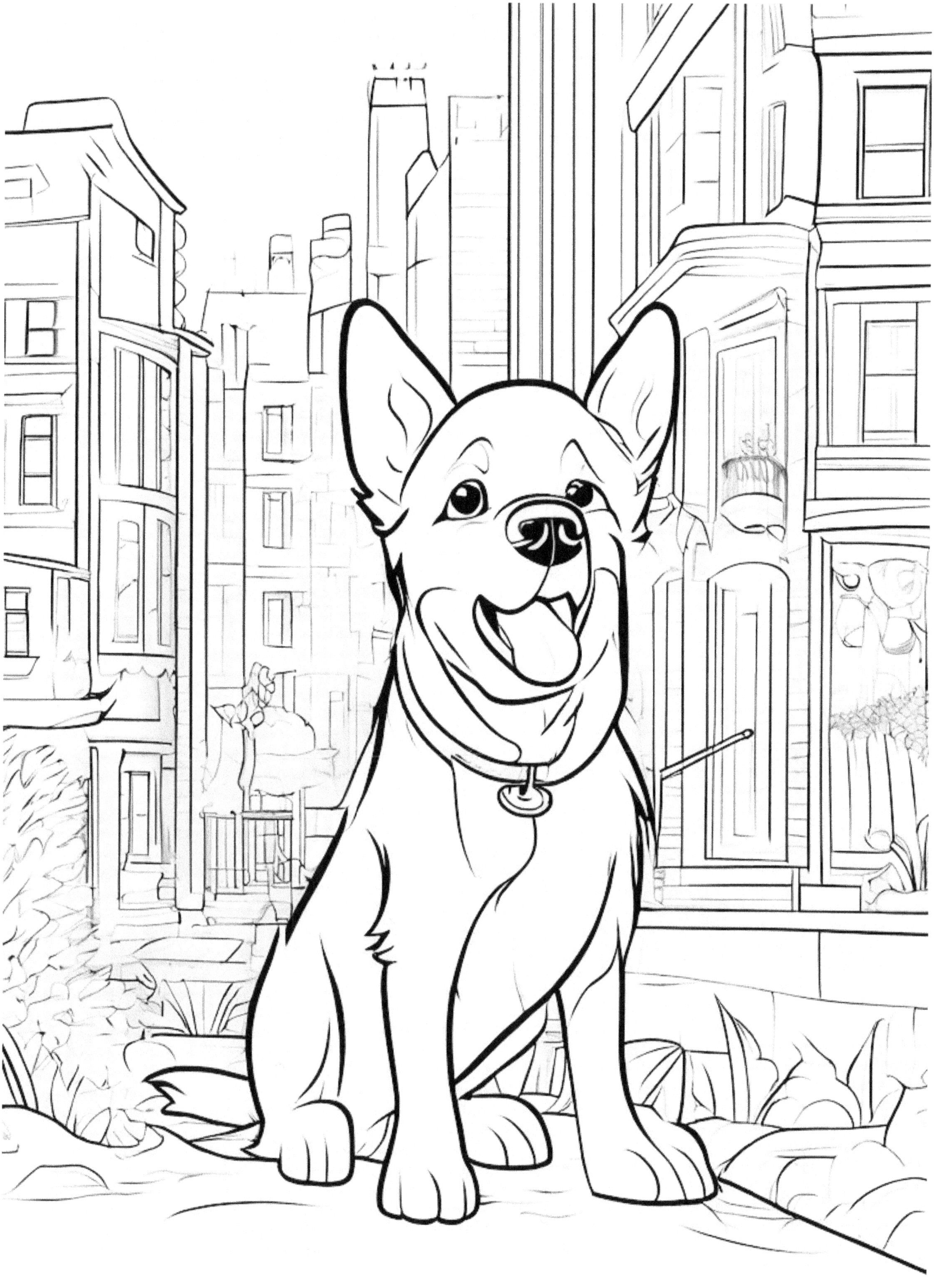

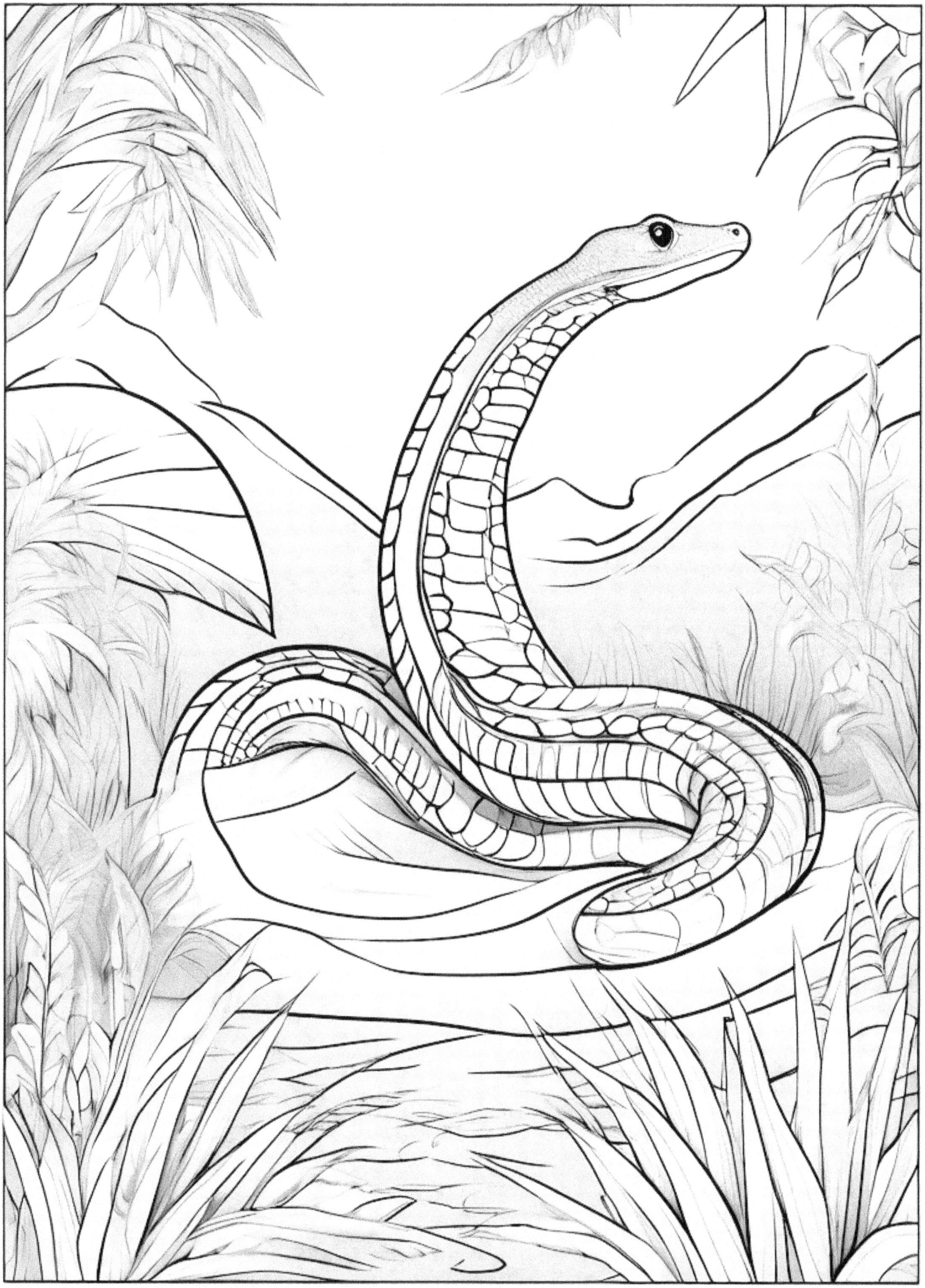

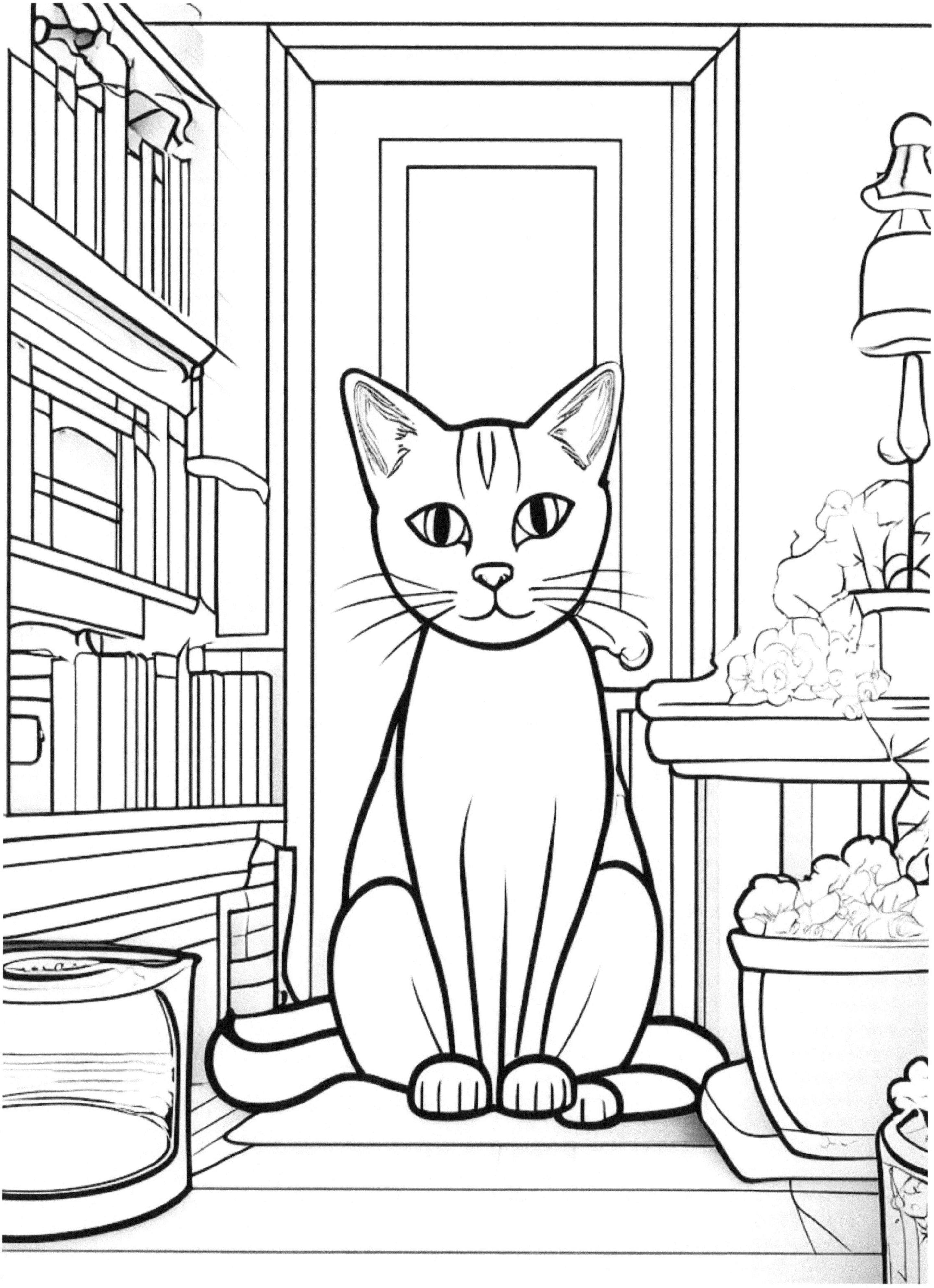

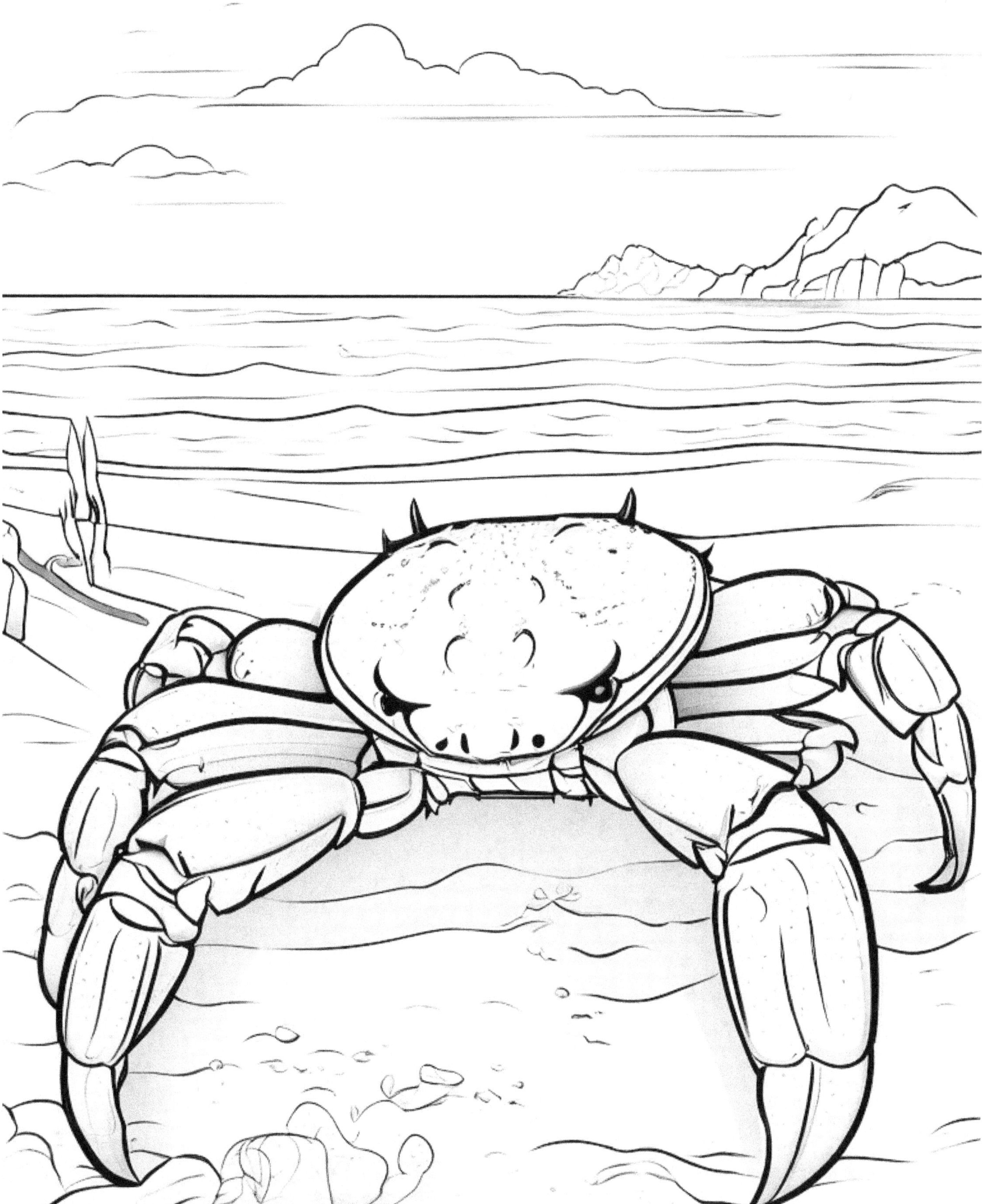

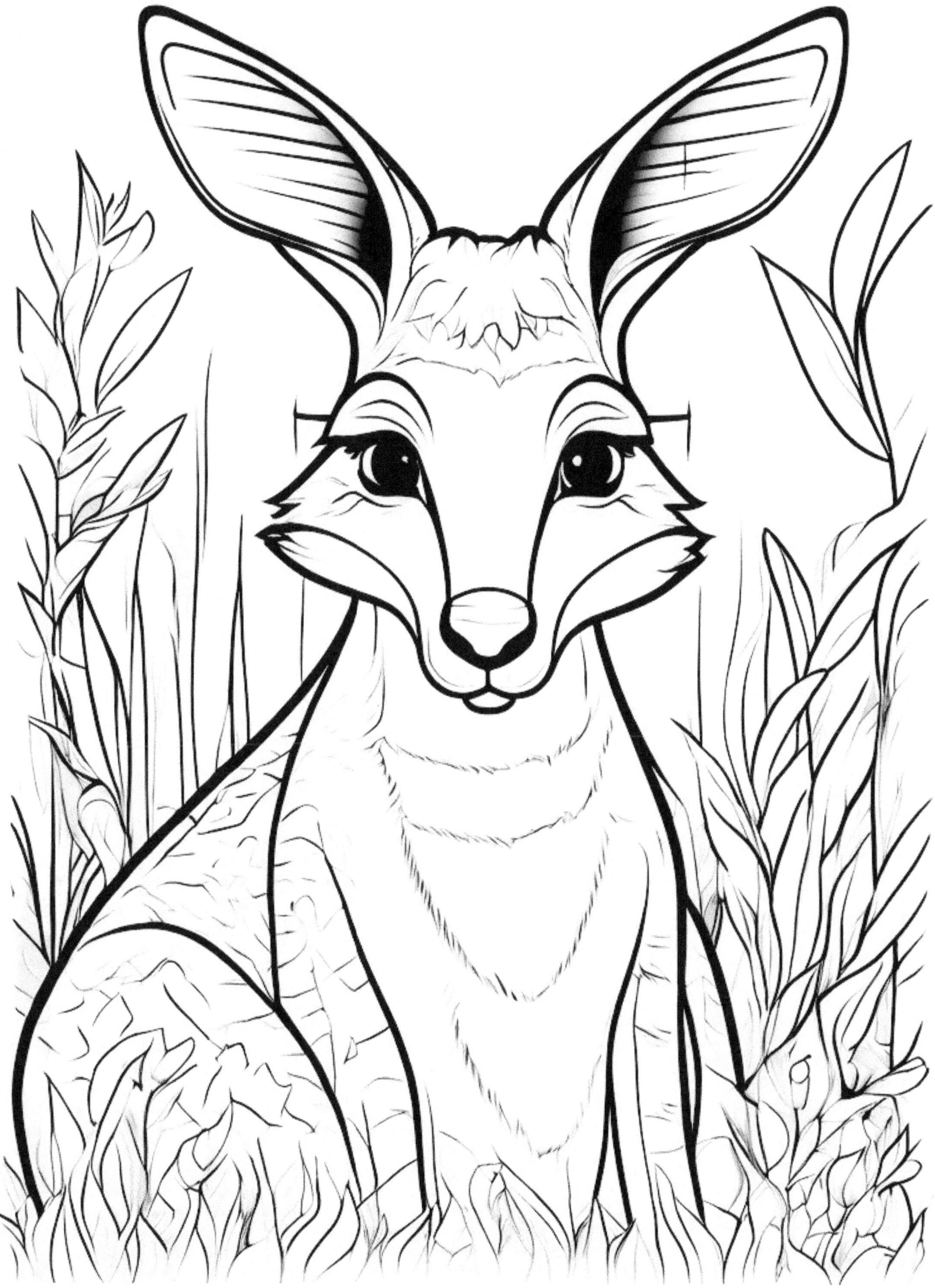

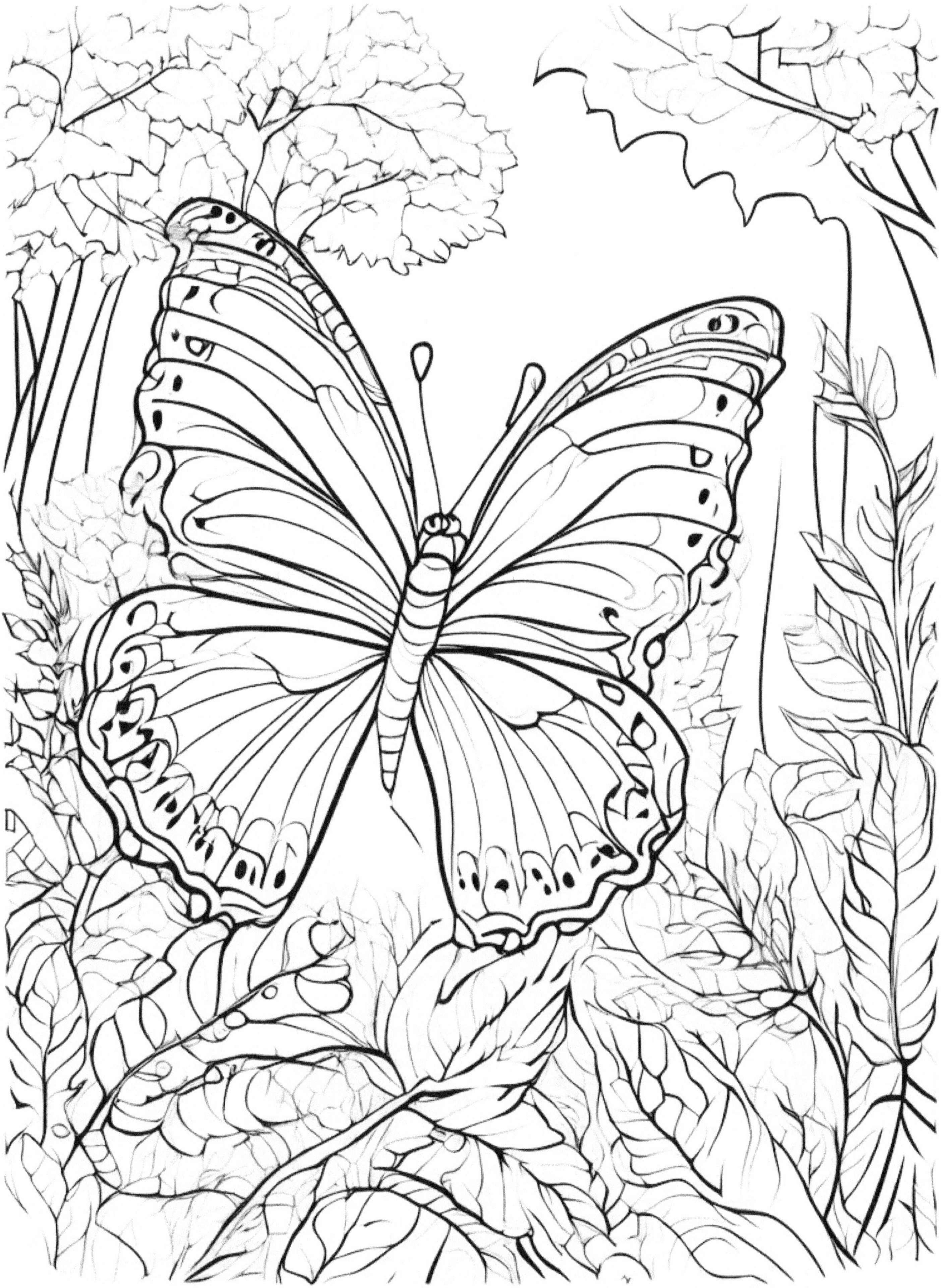

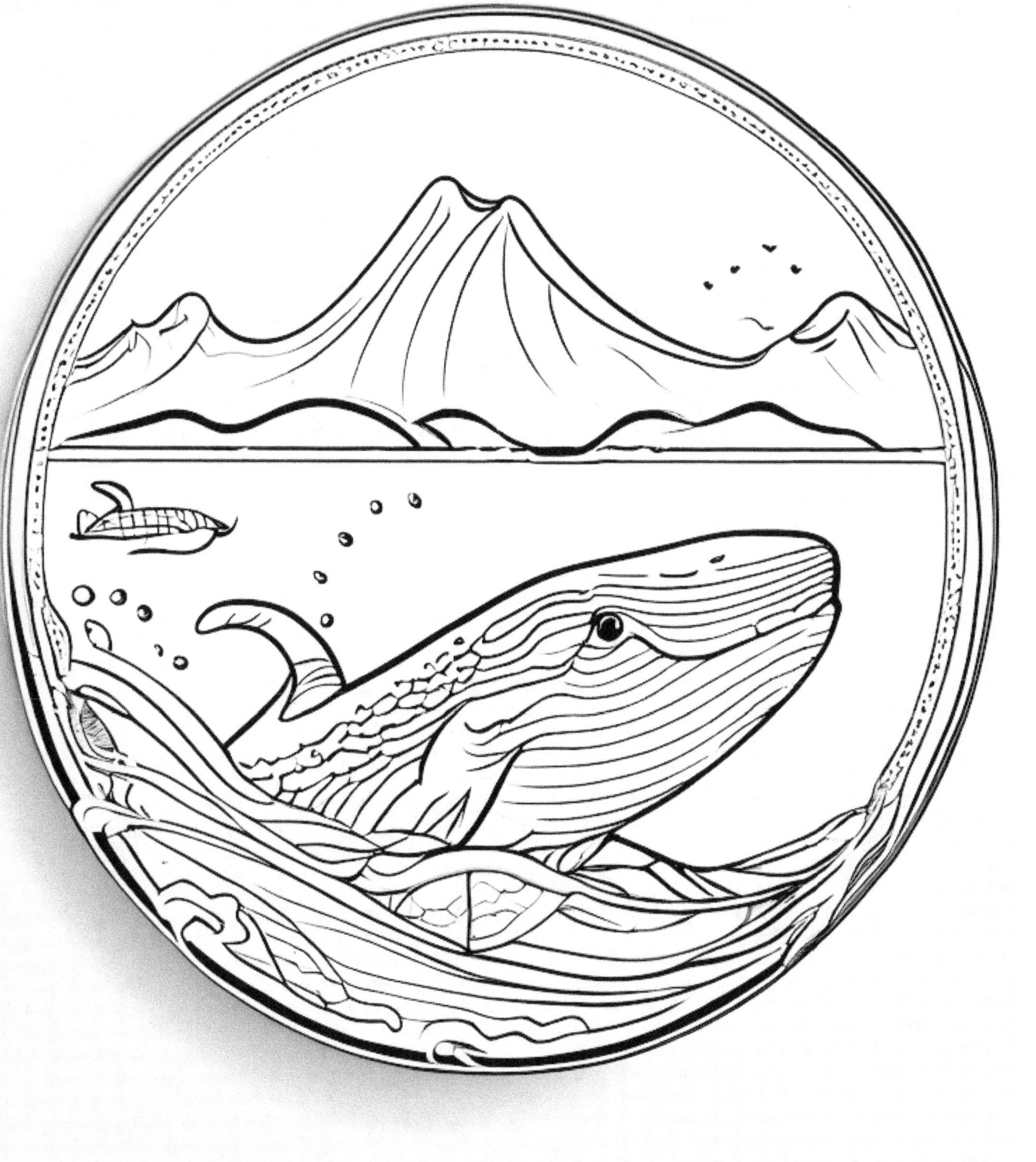

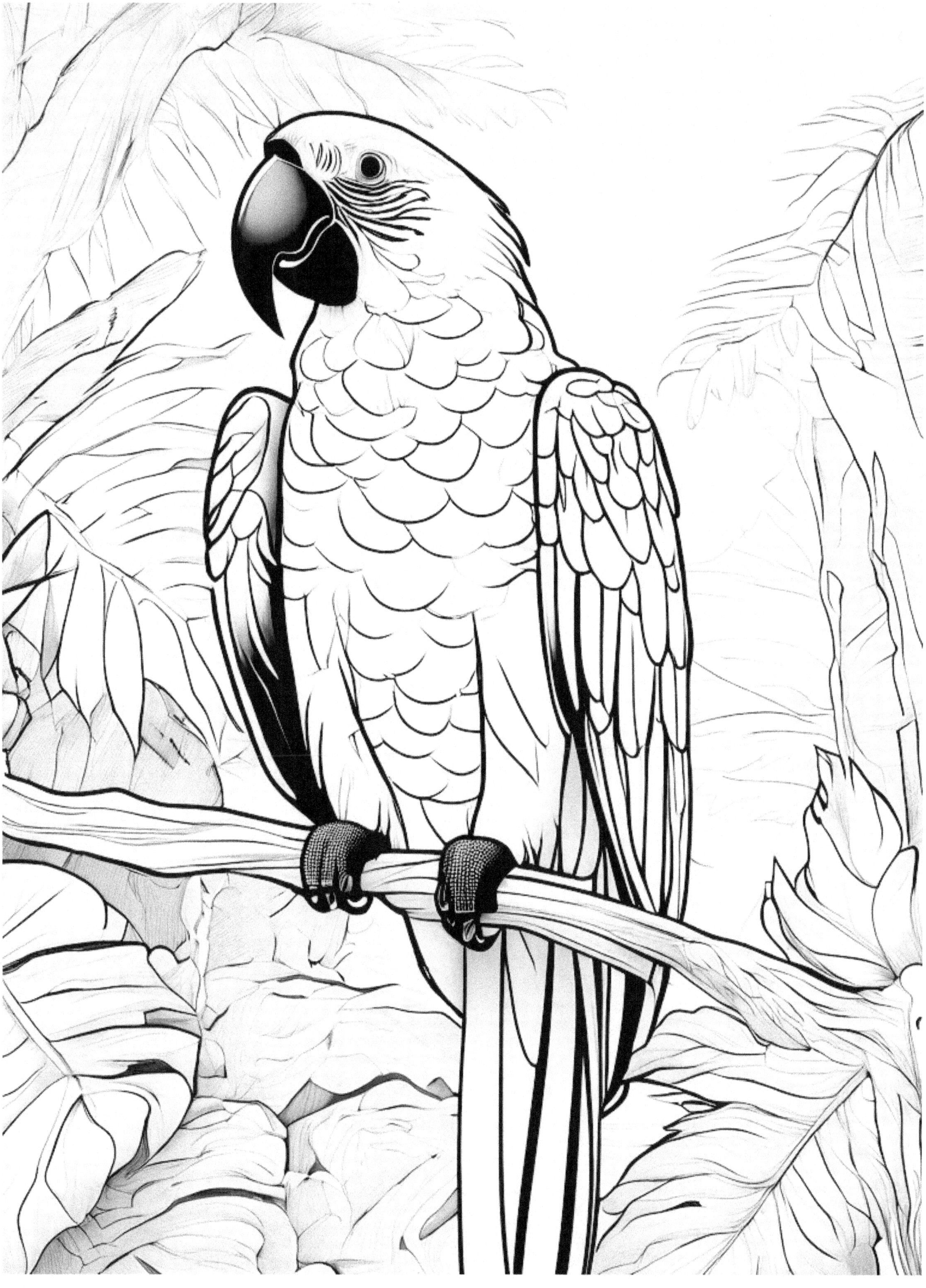

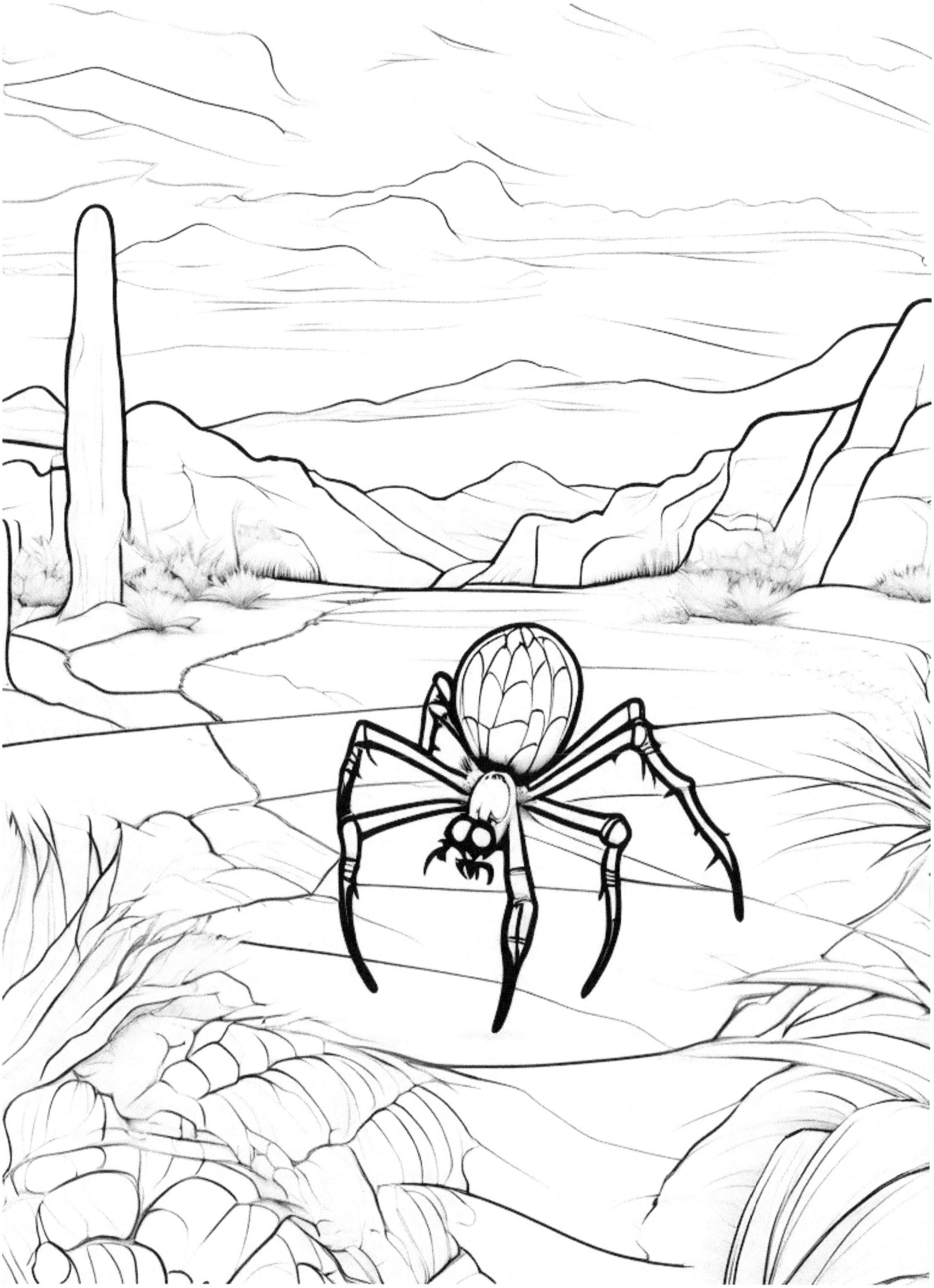

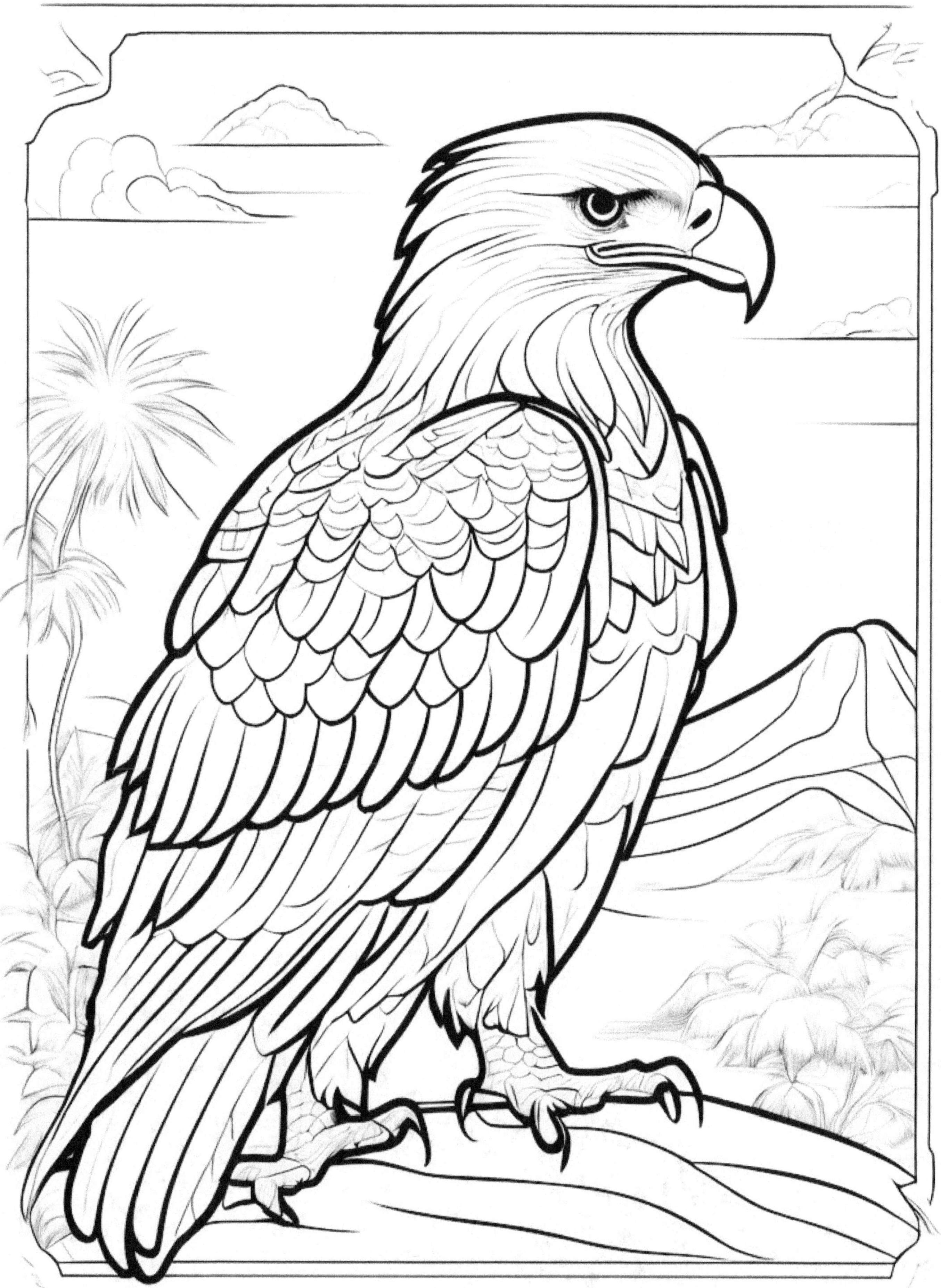

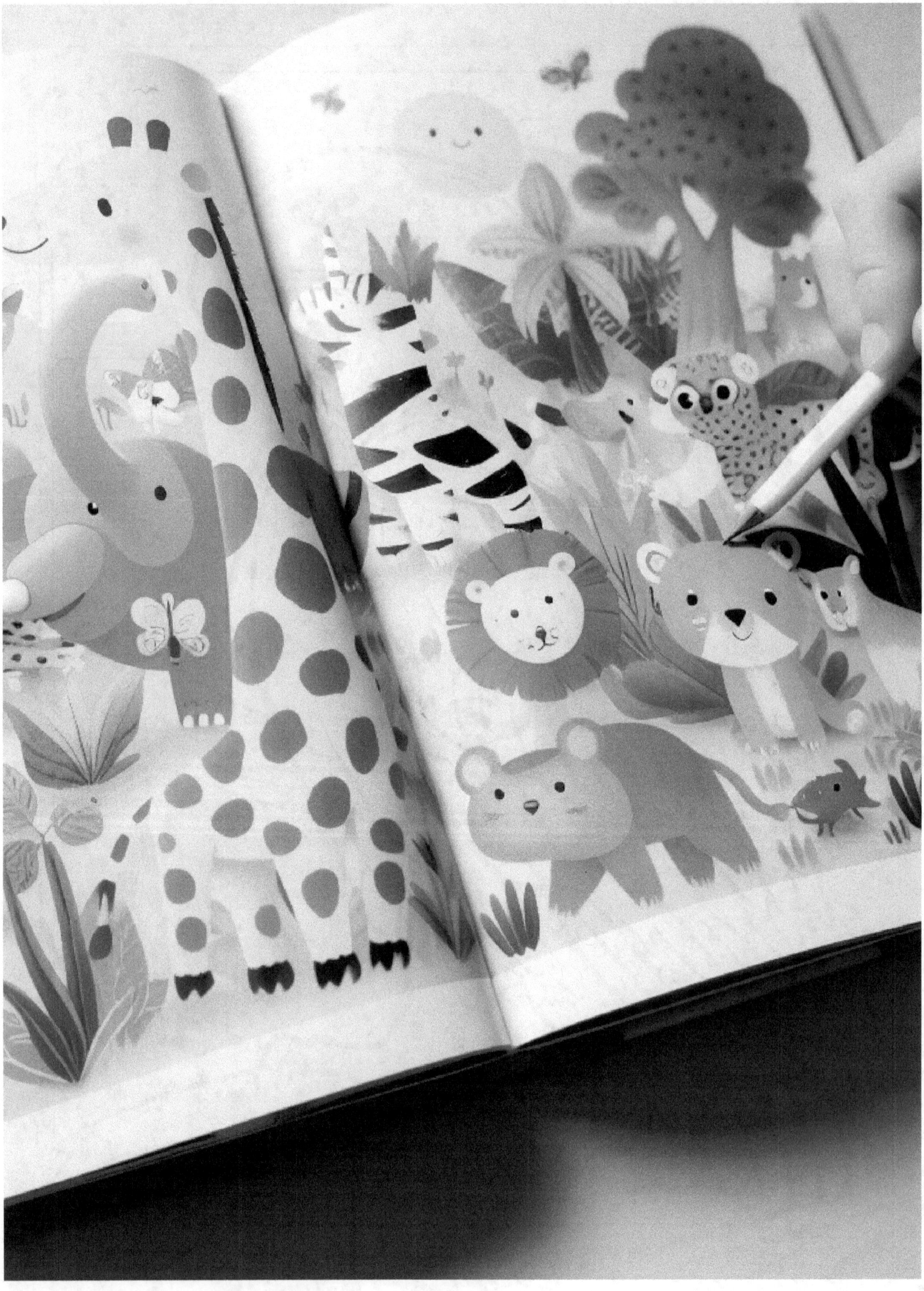

www.ingramcontent.com/pod-product-compliance
Lightning Source LLC
Chambersburg PA
CBHW081204290526
45796CB00010B/335
* 9 7 9 8 8 7 6 5 2 4 5 3 9 *